Broken Little Flowers: A Decade Devoted to Putting Pedophiles Behind Bars

Christian Guth

Published by Christian Guth, 2024.

BROKEN LITTLE FLOWERS: A DECADE DEVOTED TO PUTTING PEDOPHILES BEHIND BARS

First edition. May 7, 2024.

Copyright © 2024 Christian Guth.

ISBN: 979-8224356638

Written by Christian Guth.

Table of Contents

Preface 1

Introduction 11

I - 2000, Year One of the Fight Against Child Sexual Abuse 15

II - The Ogre of Sihanoukville 31

III - The Pedophile of the Woods 39

IV - Such a Sweet Professor 47

V - Little Flowers – Part One 55

VI - Little Flowers – Part Two 61

VII - Letters to Nary, Sokha, Chen, Pech, Oeun, May, Bopha and Sophea 69

VIII - On the Trail of Human Traffickers 83

IX - The Tiger Takes a Fall 105

X - "Junge, komm bald wieder" 121

XI - Non-Governmental Organizations: Essential but Sometimes a Hindrance 137

XII - A Plea for the Regulation of Prostitution 151

Conclusion 165

Acknowledgements 175

Translator's Acknowledgements 177

To my Cambodian and expatriate friends, and to this country so dear to my heart – you have given me so much, taught me so much! I will always remember the colorful, at times spellbinding images, the delicious flavors, the kaleidoscope of emotions and most of all, the smiles of a thousand facets.

Preface

This is the story of how I spent ten years fighting sexual exploitation of children and putting pedophiles, rapists and child traffickers behind bars. This took place in what had been considered a "paradise" for pedophiles: Cambodia, right after its wars and genocides had finally ended. In a land reeling from that sort of chaos, children were easy prey.

I first went to Cambodia to work at the French Embassy in 1994, never imagining I would remain there sixteen years, and fulfill what turned out to be some of the most important missions of my life, especially those last ten years, when I helped set up and oversee a police network to fight sexual exploitation of children.

Like most people disembarking in Cambodia's capital Phnom Penh back then, I knew about the terrible suffering this small Southeast Asian kingdom had endured under the thumb of Pol Pot and his Khmer Rouge soldiers. It was one of the worst tragedies in human history. Between 1975 and 1979, these communist fanatics left hundreds of thousands of corpses behind them, buried in mass graves throughout the country, all in the name of some supposed utopia they would build from the ashes in a new world.

The Khmer Rouge executed between one and two million people. With the disease and starvation caused by their rule, as many as four million people died, while countless others were reduced to slavery. Intellectuals were eliminated, religion banned, "family" suppressed, money abolished, schools closed, farmland collectivized, state institutions – including the courts and police – and the pre-war industrial base destroyed. An unparalleled genocide.

And the Cambodians' ordeal did not end when Vietnamese troops entered Phnom Penh on January 7, 1979, to "liberate" the country. The troops did force the Pol Potists to withdraw their soldiers into the northwestern area astride the border with Thailand, but the country was caught in the vise of the Cold

War and the rivalries roiling the Communist bloc. Cambodia joined the Soviet camp and placed its civil and military plans under the tutelage of Vietnam. This resulted in an international embargo that condemned the nation to ten long years of underdevelopment and destitution.

And the Khmer Rouge? They may have been defeated, but they were not eliminated. Hoping to retake Phnom Penh, they were forever on the offensive, besieging the military positions of the Hanoi-supported local government, whose mainstay was the Communist Party of Kampuchea. This later evolved into the Cambodian People's Party (CCP), which remains in power to this day. The members changed the name in 1991 during a peace and reconciliation process, as a sign the country would abandon Marxist-Leninist ideology and open up to the economic ways of the Western world.

After the Berlin Wall fell in 1989 and the Paris Peace Accords were signed in 1991, those hopes of normalization and a return to a decent life finally resurfaced. But the fallout from all those years of horror and civil war would take many years, even decades, to be eradicated. I realized this my first night in Phnom Penh, when I walked through its crumbling, deserted roads.

It gets dark early there, around 6 pm, and with no lighting in the streets, people did not go out, even though the curfew didn't fall until 9 pm. I didn't know it at the time, but they were too scared to go out if it wasn't absolutely necessary.

Only a few scattered shops were open, shedding glaring light into roads full of rubble, with rats skittering here and there and a few wandering dogs. A city that seemed dead. But this city dreamed of rebirth and a better existence, akin to how Buddhism teaches one to hope no matter how baseless it may seem. A profound desire for freedom and regrowth was lighting the horizons of this ruined nation.

The elections of 1993, organized under the auspices of the United Nations, ushered in a government headed by the FUNCINPEC[1], at least in name. This party won the popular vote, but was dominated by the CCP, creating a two-headed institutional aberration only Khmer[2] politicians could invent, with a FUNCINPEC first Prime Minister and a CCP second Prime Minister, each having to approve all decisions. This duplication repeated itself in all the nation's institutions, provincial and central. And although Cambodia recognized King Norodom Sihanouk with decorum and traditional festivities, the CCP party exercised the real power of government.

Cambodia was one of the poorest countries in the world at that time, heavily dependent on international aid to keep afloat. But a large part of the millions of dollars[3] pouring in every year ended up feeding corruption, and state institutions were often left without a penny in funding to fulfill their goals. The entire situation on the ground was still very unstable, with sporadic fighting in the streets – I could hear guns sounding tchak-tchak-tchak at times. There was no water clean enough to drink, and every day, the electricity would go out for a few hours or many hours. The noise and fumes produced by generators was constant. All the roads were in shambles. Between the armies' mining operations and the civilians' use of mines – anyone could buy them at local markets to "protect" their fields from thieves – there were mines everywhere (and are still being stepped on, to the anguish of Cambodian families). Procuring the basic necessities of life, especially for a Westerner, was complicated, and "comfort" became a relative term.

This was the reality of Cambodia when I arrived in May 1994.

From then until the end of 1998, while remaining an officer of France's International Technical Police Cooperation, I worked as the French Embassy's "Law Enforcement Advisor to the Cambodian Ministry of the Interior." I'd been selected because of my wide-ranging experience as a police commander. During many years in African hotspots, I had dealt with terrorism, drug enforcement, judicial corruption and other difficult assignments apt to bring an officer into violent confrontations.

The Ministry of the Interior governs the Cambodian National Police, the police academy and upper-level officer training, including intelligence agencies and judicial police, and its various branches, like the anti-drug squad and immigration police. The National Police had just reinstated this advisory position I was to fill. It had been discontinued in 1975 when the Khmer Rouge took power, but now they needed someone to develop and strengthen processes within the police branches and develop their superior officers' skills through training.

The embassy and my superiors in Paris entrusted me with three missions.

My first task was to organize and run training programs for more than a hundred officers who led criminal investigation departments in the capital and the provinces. Most of them came from the ranks of the liberation army, but some of the older ones had served with the police before 1975. They had little or no formal training in criminal law, procedure or investigative techniques, having gotten all their experience in the field. I was to bring them up to snuff in the necessary legal knowledge and know-how and, through role play and case studies, teach them to adapt their behavior to international ethical standards of the profession. And I had limited time to do it, as the officers alternated active duty with training, so I could give each officer only four months training in total. The government considered that sufficient, especially since it would be followed by specialized training sessions. When I first took on the task, it was with a sinking feeling. To assess the current situation and levels of training needed, I would have to travel out to the provinces, and knowing it was so dangerous there in the capital, I could only imagine how bad it was in the rest of that devastated country. But I carried out my mission and lived to tell the tale.

The second operation involved creating a Narcotics Bureau, which quickly got excellent results despite technical difficulties and, as diplomats say, "local constraints." In other words, powerful elites, clans, religious and traditional beliefs such as "karma," and above all, corruption. All of which impeded our police work, even if at that time, Cambodia was more of a drug transit country, with only a bit of marijuana production and very little consumption of drugs.

My third task was as unexpected as it was uncommon. I was to create a Heritage Police Unit responsible for protecting the principal Angkor[4] temples in the Siem Reap[5] region. After the entire site had been completely demined, armed pillagers repeatedly attacked the temples, using sledgehammers and chisels to pry off pieces of carved stone, and then selling them as antiquities. They had caused considerable damage to this multi-secular temple complex, now considered the eighth Wonder of the World, even beating Italy's Pompeii.

The Heritage Police were to put a stop to this desecration. After training personnel and establishing thirty surveillance posts, we set up an investigative and research unit on a national level and formed motorcycle patrols to intervene rapidly on archeological sites as necessary. I monitored the operation of these services and supervised training techniques to enhance the project.

Nevertheless, our commitment had to be put on hold midway. The country entered a highly unstable period beginning in July 1997, when violent clashes erupted between the CCP forces and those of the royalists assisted by Khmer Rouge units. Then came the post-election protests of 1998. All this upheaval brought a stop to my Heritage Unit training sessions, and my mission was reoriented toward "following the situation's evolution." In other words, to engage in intelligence work for the French Embassy.

My many contacts and my close relationships with administrators who wanted to help the country and its people gave me an "ears to the ground" perspective appreciated by the French ambassador, who used it to help define his position toward the complex, dangerous situation Cambodia found itself in, and to devise a strategy. At that time, France's voice still accounted for much there. Since the United Nations Transitional Authority in Cambodia (UNTAC) troops had departed at the end of 1993, the former French protectorate had benefited from the technical help of French advisors connected to the main ministers. Like my own role to work with the Minister of the Interior, other counselors were hired to work with other ministries.

After four and a half years, I reached the end of my contract. I was now in my fifties and thinking about retirement, but the idea of winding up my career in some desk job back in France did not appeal to me. I wanted to remain in Cambodia, a land whose emotional power had seduced me. I was well aware of its drawbacks, especially the excessive violence people often chose to resolve private or societal conflicts, but I felt I would be more useful there than in France, where my on-the-ground work experience in every part of the globe would serve no purpose – so many other colleagues could occupy the kind of post I would be offered.

I could have entered the private sector, always looking to hire former cops, and the market was booming for bodyguards. A large security company as well as a French bank offered me senior security positions, but I wanted more than that. Spending my days organizing work schedules for a team of guards was not an option for me, I decided. I wanted to use my professional skills, and to keep developing them, and only an "open season on fresh adventure" would provide that.

What I sought was a new commitment, one that would fulfill my dream of using my law enforcement expertise to serve the people who most needed help, and Cambodia was full of them. I especially wanted to help, in a direct and concrete way, the weakest members of its society: children and other vulnerable people.

While still working at the French Embassy, I helped the Cambodian police find and arrest French child molesters on two occasions, and I'd been astonished to learn that no Western nation had established, or even envisaged, any police cooperation programs there for the protection of children. I figured the subject was too sensitive. Addressing it meant confronting many potent elements in Cambodian society: influential officials in the army, the police, and the courts, but also powerful, rich businessmen linked to corruption. Any official program to tackle child sexual exploitation risked failing.

There would undoubtedly be conflicts with people involved in investigations, pressure to prevent them from achieving their goals, the possibility of traitors within the organization itself who would inform traffickers, exploiters or sexual offenders of any ongoing investigations, and scandals could arise if anyone involved in the program was denounced in the media for being a pimp or for protecting pimps, pedophiles or traffickers. It was a long and daunting list.

But children were such easy prey in a country undermined by poverty, corruption and shaky government institutions, practically all of which were compromised, especially the judicial system. The most vulnerable members of society were surrounded by a thousand dangers: sexual predators, especially pedophiles, attracted by Cambodia's reputation as a rich "hunting ground," prostitution, no-fuss adoption rings, trafficking, sweat shops and so on.

But before exploring how I could join the fight to help children there, I returned to Paris to check in with my department (International Technical Police Cooperation). That experience only bolstered my desire to keep working in Cambodia.

When I met with my chief of staff, he offered me a post leading a training unit. Although this was technically a promotion, his indifference to my skills and experience as a police commander left me feeling bitter. I had always done my work with determination and strength. I had fulfilled all my missions. But there was no word of congratulations for my distinguished career, which I felt merited it. Nothing. It's true, I had only done the work I was paid for, and the chief must have thought the satisfaction of a job well done in my chosen career was sufficient compensation.

I left the interview thinking, "I'll create my own mission this time, my last, the one I'll be most proud of and most want to remember and talk about."

After a few weeks in France visiting family and taking care of paperwork, I returned to Cambodia. I tested a few jobs in the private sector, but they didn't motivate me, so I traveled a while through Myanmar, Laos, Malaysia and many other countries for meetings, job interviews and simply to learn more about Southeast Asia as a whole. Cambodia remained my home port though.

During my wanderings, I came to realize my goal was not only to help rescue sex crime victims, both women and children, but to fight against their aggressors, no matter who they were. They needed to be punished, to be locked up in prison. I decided to turn the page and become a consultant, a free agent. I felt committed to working in dangerous territory, in every sense of the term, where only a few courageous NGOs had dared to venture.

I was far from imagining how all this would take form, but somehow, I knew it would materialize if I searched long enough. And so it proved: I heard of the perfect opportunity to fight these sexual predators and I seized it, becoming International Police Advisor to head the Law Enforcement Against Sexual Exploitation and Trafficking of Children (LEASETC) Project[6]. My chance had come.

The Cambodian Ministry of the Interior and UNICEF launched this project together, and their goal was to improve the national police's ability to investigate and rescue victims of these kinds of crimes, and especially to arrest and convict the perpetrators. It would be an uphill battle, and for me personally, a profound experience that taught me a great deal professionally and emotionally.

In this book, I recount the first 10 years of that project. This narrative also serves to prove that when a society and its police force stand up and rally for the victims of sexual crimes, especially children, they can protect them and ensure they are treated justly. It's too easy to say a cause is lost in advance simply because the road to success is steep and studded with obstacles and traps. Sometimes, all that's needed is a spark to awaken people's energy and buried abilities. We create that spark by gathering existing talent, then organizing the fight through a medium of special units with well-adapted means and new professional skills. And it was urgent to act – so many victims were crying out for help, and the offenders could no longer go unpunished.

The fact this project succeeded beyond anyone's expectations, to the point that we were bringing some 700 indictments a year by the end of that decade, shows it can work anywhere in the world. Achieving results like that in a country such as Cambodia, a "ground zero" for sexual exploitation of children, where we had to build a specialized department from the ground-up, proves that it can work elsewhere in Asia, and in fact, in any country where a system to battle this crime does not yet exist.

I'm proud of having worked with the Cambodian police assigned to this effort. Day in and day out, I measured not only their rapid progress in mastering the skills needed for this work, but also their integrity and commitment, drastically different from the far too many corrupt Cambodian police officers who dishonored and discredited their profession among their own people and in the eyes of the international community, there and abroad.

Like the phoenix, Cambodia was reborn from the ashes after so many years of war and suffering. Part of its rebirth entailed taking action against the scourge of exploitation, sexual abuse, and trafficking of children. I feel confident it will make the necessary efforts to continue the fight.

Introduction

Sex Tourism and Crimes Against Children in Cambodia

As we all know, sex sells. During the 1990s and the early 2000s, international reporters passing through Phnom Penh routinely covered the Khmer Rouge and the ceaseless corruption, disorder, and predicaments of Cambodian politics, and they also turned in the obligatory article about "sex tourism," with a particular focus on the pedophiles operating with impunity throughout the country.

A poor nation, with its social structures torn to ribbons after years of civil war, Cambodia had become a rich hunting ground for pedophiles because so many children lived on the streets or "worked" in brothels. Cambodia figured among the top ten in the list of favorite destinations for international sex predators, as is witnessed by the countless cases taken up by the police and the LEASETC Project since its creation in 2000.

To make it clear right away, the word "pedophile" used throughout this book means "pedocriminal," for the person in question here cannot in any case be considered a child's "friend," even if many invoke that excuse to justify their acts. No, they are sex offenders, criminals whose victims are children.

In 1995, Margaret de Monchy, the woman responsible for UNICEF's local program for 'children in especially difficult circumstances,' remarked in an interview for the French language newspaper *Cambodge Soir* that "foreign pedophiles represent a genuine danger to Cambodia."

This may surprise people, but there is another type of sex tourist, one not viewed as a dangerous criminal. That would be the ordinary sex tourist who comes to Asia to hire consenting adults for sex. The key word is "adults." Because he (or she, but we'll continue using the masculine pronoun) is not committing a heinous crime, he is of no particular interest to criminal investigators.

This kind of occasional traveler is drawn to Asia because, reputedly, it's easier to satisfy his sexual fantasies there, and at a lower cost. Mostly married men, they usually travel alone, as a duo, or in a small group. These seemingly respectable visitors "want to have a good time" for the duration of a short trip, and they let themselves be tempted by opportunities. Far from home and disapproving neighbors, colleagues or spouses, far from the moral values and norms of their native land, they profess to believe that in places like Cambodia, uninhibited sexuality is normal and paying for sex at the "market price" causes no harm. On the contrary, they assume their paid partners were born into a life of conflict and poverty, and that hiring them improves their quality of life. These justifications appear trivial, but for sex tourists, they suffice in order to enjoy, guilt-free, their escapades in Cambodia, the "Land of Smiles."

This category of sex tourist usually sticks to "acceptable" prostitution – consensual and without sexual exploitation of minors – and they generally escape the arm of justice in countries like Cambodia or Thailand, where prostitution is illegal but tolerated. But sometimes these customers do engage in sexual acts with minors, deliberately or not. Maybe they drank too much to know the difference or were encouraged or sheltered by a *mama-san*.[7] But whether it happened only once, "by accident" or not, they are still considered child abusers and must be brought before the courts.

Then there are sex tourists of a different type, pedophiles, the ones Margaret de Monchy denounced as a genuine danger. These predators prepare their trips in advance, sometimes with the help of special agencies who arrange every detail according to the type of sexual relations they prefer, with very young "partners," boys or girls. Here we find true child molesters attracted exclusively to children, as well as people who may not usually exhibit sexual behavior of that nature, but still seek relations with "adults with youthful traits," who are in fact children ranging in age from 12 to 15 years old.

In Asia, these "informed" tourists, who come from every social category and age group, try to convince themselves and others that the prostitution of minors is carried on in a gentle, almost innocent fashion, and even with the child's consent. But in the Cambodia I knew, that of the 1990s and 2000s, the reality was entirely different. Many young prostitutes, especially the younger girls, were sold to brothels as virgins, then raped and repeatedly resold, exploited as sex objects in the prostitution network, and often beaten, even tortured.

And where did these girls come from? Most came from uninformed families, who delivered their own children to prostitution bosses. People were bereft of social protection then, and were pushed by poverty or duped by pimps, to whom they might have owed money, a typical scheme, thus furnishing an endless supply of "raw material" and allowing this scandalous, insufferable industry to continue. Once the trap snapped shut on the young victims, their futures were sealed, and only a pitiful few ever managed to free themselves by their own efforts.

During the time I worked on the LEASETC Project, most global press coverage about pedophiles in Cambodia implicated tourists from Western countries, so people around the world thought this type of crime was imported from the West – a falsehood that suited local authorities just fine. Although the number of Westerners interested in young Cambodian girls or "street boys" increased throughout the years, our team of investigators discovered that Cambodian and Chinese pedocriminals were responsible for most child molestations and rapes.

All these predators – Asian or Western – were well aware of the extreme poverty of a great part of Cambodia's population and of the weakness and corruption of the local justice system. They figured they could find satisfaction there without running too many risks.

I will return later to the idea of "acceptable" prostitution of adults, but that of children is never acceptable – no argument possible. Children cannot be considered prostitutes, because they have no power, even relative, to choose to accept or refuse to have sex with another person. No, they are victims of sexual exploitation by the "client" and anyone else profiting from it.

In many criminal cases outside the prostitution circuits, the pedophile poses as a protector of children from poor families who could not even feed or clothe them. But let it be said once and for all: when an adult has sexual relations with children, no matter the context, he destroys their lives and futures, and makes accomplices of every person involved in the crime, including those who bought the children, who ripped them from their families' arms, and who raped, beat or sold them.

I - 2000, Year One of the Fight Against Child Sexual Abuse

Before the year 2000, the Cambodian police made no effort to protect minors from sexual exploitation. None. Rather succinct, but there's no other way to describe it.

I don't mean to condemn the Cambodian police outright, as there were many extenuating circumstances. Until the end of the 1990s, armed groups of Khmer Rouge were still roaming the country, and most Cambodians, traumatized by the unspeakable horrors they had endured under Pol Pot, were preoccupied with basic needs like food and shelter.

The authorities' number one task was protecting the peace and ensuring the safety of civilians. Beyond that stretched a long road, to rebuild a police force that respected the conventions of international law, and addressed all the needs of its citizens. Their first step was to create the multidisciplinary structure required for basic services: ensuring public and road safety, protecting property, guarding people against all forms of crime, maintaining order. Then, slowly but surely, special services were incorporated in order of priority. Did the fight against drugs and the pillaging of their patrimony take priority over the trafficking and sexual abuse of children? I would like to say "No!" but I can't. However, I understood the government's urgency to overhaul every department of the police force.

They did place the fight against child sexual exploitation fairly high on the agenda, though, partly because it was a subject of major concern in international cooperation, in particular among International Organizations (IOs) and their member states. Headed by Western countries at that time, this IO community had enormous influence on the government's decisions, seeing as how they allocated hundreds of millions of dollars to Cambodia every year. Taking that and national political factors into account, child trafficking became a flashpoint, especially after the World Congress in Stockholm in August 1996.

Cambodia was being described in the global media as a kind of Wild West where pedophiles were swarming in from around the globe. The police force had to respond, but it found itself in new territory, with no experience or set procedures to fight this insidious, nearly invisible crime, which had not yet even been judged "highest priority."

But then UNICEF and several other international organizations joined hands with the Cambodian Ministry of the Interior to create the LEASETC support project.

I would spend the next decade, from 2000 to 2010, as its consultant and overseer. I was posted on the front line, given the task of forming a new investigative department from scratch, whose necessity would be proved only if its results were convincing and rapid. That piled the pressure on.

My intimate knowledge of the Ministry of the Interior's mysteries and the support of the police high command played in my favor for getting hired, although that very closeness had nearly knocked me out of the running. Many members of the police hierarchy had been my criminal investigation students when I'd been working for the French cooperation service, and that made me seem suspicious to certain backers.

"Won't he take the police's side if they decide to stifle cases?" people asked. "After all, everyone knows how corrupt they are."

I convinced them that on the contrary, without that closeness, without that confidence the upper levels had in me, the project would go nowhere, and that would be to the detriment of Cambodian children. We had to be able to immediately fit into the policing system to become efficient in a short time.

What happened next proved me right.

To this day, the name Hok Lundy still brings shivers to any Cambodian older than 50, even though he died when his helicopter crashed in 2008. Until then, Hok Lundy was the powerful commander of the national police, and according to rumor – the main source of information at that time – this made him responsible for many disappearances, each more horrific than the last.

Like the Cambodian People's Party and other hierarchies of power, Hok Lundy came back to life after the long, pitiless war. He hadn't survived it by showering his enemies with roses. And bizarrely enough, this man ended up as the Project's key contact person; his confidence in us and in the Project were indispensable if it were to move forward. If we needed something, Hok Lundy made sure we got it. He did not support us for personal reasons or out of the kindness of his heart, but because he wanted to improve his reputation with the people, so it was in both of our interests to work together, a "win-win" situation.

It was also in the interest of the government to push this project. To improve Cambodia's image on the international stage, it needed to show progress at all levels, not only economic but social and humanitarian. By convincing the Ministry of the Interior officials to join UNICEF in the global movement against child trafficking and sexual exploitation, the administration burnished its image. This acted in the interest of our goals, and ultimately in the interest of the children.

I believe in the heroism of balance, not in the heroism of the exceptional, which, except in rare instances, exists only in Hollywood films: one person, alone, battling against a hundred to save a handful of victims. That makes for a good movie plot and ticket sales, but in the real world, a vicious world, multifaceted heroism and a well-controlled balancing act succeeds far better at uniting disparate, even antagonistic forces to work toward a common goal. My kind of hero is an ordinary person who leads other ordinary people to join in his or her actions, not simply admire them. Occasional failures are certain, but we learn, we gain confidence and succeed more and more often. The Project flourished thanks to "heroes" like the many police officers devoted to their mission during my years of work with the various law enforcement services.

The IOs supporting the Project and the Minister of the Interior signed a memorandum of understanding, and the Project was launched, with an average yearly budget of $300,000 dollars. Most of the prominent leaders in the national police supported it.

Secretary of State Prum Sokha became Chairman of the Project Coordination Committee, filling a primordial role as central authority on the Cambodian side. He represented the Minister and the government itself. His support never once flagged. We trusted each other, and I could always count on his encouragement during our regular meetings to monitor the project's progress. Without him, the Project could never have gotten off the ground. And it was Prum Sokha who convinced Hok Lundy to extend his crucial support and guarantee the willing involvement of the national police.

The government and the IOs agreed to divide costs equally, with the IOs giving cash, while the Ministry provided headquarters, administration, and human resources. I immediately started hiring to form a core group of men and women with the energy and capabilities to make the Project a success. All of them belonged to the CPP, the ruling party, as did nearly everyone else who joined us over the years. The country was structured that way in the 2000s, with the police and armed forces under its exclusive control, and nothing has changed since then.

I carefully considered my hiring choices. When I suggested a number of my most motivated former interns, the Ministry agreed, and signed on a few others, among them a woman, General Un Sokunthea. She was appointed to lead the anti-human trafficking and juvenile protection department (AHTJP), developed hand in hand with the Project. Hiring a woman signaled to me they understood certain particularities of the Project's mission. For example, she would emphasize to her staff the importance of sympathizing with the mostly female victims, and to talk to and listen to them with a sincere willingness to protect them. That would be an improvement on the state of affairs that existed then, especially in interviewing child victims.

Without a French-Khmer interpreter, I would be powerless, so I hired Kong Sun, who had assisted me during my previous missions as adviser within the international Police Cooperation agency. He immediately accepted when I asked him to join this second adventure. Small and energetic, he had one particularity I will always remember: He was gifted with a perfect set of teeth, which he meticulously cleaned after eating by jetting water out between his teeth, talking all the while, then, if necessary, by picking at them with a toothpick or any available twig. I became somewhat fluent in Khmer later on, and was at ease with English, but Sun had many other things to teach me besides how to clean my teeth the Cambodian way. Imbued with Buddhism, his ever-optimistic view of human existence impressed me so profoundly that Buddhism came to influence my comprehension of daily life and its trials.

A former teacher and interpreter, Sun had survived the Khmer Rouge by hiding his profession and his knowledge of French, and passing for a farm worker. He shared impressions of that time as if it were another life, never trying to gain sympathy.

"Westerners talk a lot about the past and the future," he would say. "Why? We can't change the past. The parents we had, the events that marked us, our suffering and our joy, the good or bad decisions we've made... The past is the past. Sure, I can't forget it completely, but it shouldn't perturb my present. What counts is I'm still alive. As to the future, do we know if we'll still be alive in a year, or in a week? Do we know what our world will be like tomorrow?"

Sun's command of English was shaky, so we also needed a Khmer-English translator for communicating with the IOs' personnel. The Ministry assigned me Pich Reaksmey, a friendly young police captain who had learned English, betting correctly it would open doors for him. He was good-looking, with very dark skin that showed off his white teeth when he flashed a smile, and he was rumored to be a hit with women. Reaksmey joined our team to round out his pittance of a cop's salary, but our mission soon filled him with passion.

Just as valuable a recruit was Kim Horng, trilingual in English, French and Cambodian, and one of the first women there to earn the rank of police commander. Like Sun, she had lived through hell under the Khmer Rouge, and closed up when any mention was made of that period, but when she was with the victims of child abuse, her face always expressed compassion. Intelligent, and devoted to her country and to the Project's goals, Horng became a highly useful liaison between our team and every level of police authority.

To represent the Cambodian side of the Project, the Ministry appointed San Chhara, an administrator with the rank of Director, who would work closely with me. An excellent manager, his accounts were always correct and clear. He made sure every dollar in the budget was used for the cause we were defending and that every team member, trainer, and investigator was paid according to the rules. Punctual, elegant and ever perfectly groomed, he always wore a navy-blue dress shirt and impeccably waxed shoes. A man full of good sense, Chhara wanted to consolidate his career and build a home before marrying, which he did a few years later. His brother San Darun came to work for us too, while continuing his studies. A chauffeur at first, Darun soon became a full-fledged and well-respected member of the team.

A police officer, Pon Lin, joined us after approaching our team with a proposal to share his computer expertise. A quick-witted young man, he helped our computer technician install and adapt our criminal statistics software, and then set up our hotline and database. Lin became an integral part of the Project team through his work on the hotline, and just as he'd always wanted, he got to work hand-in-hand with major international organizations.

Completing this core group was the cheerful SreiMary[8], a police officer, wife of a police officer, and mother of two children. Srei Mary helped us with all sorts of administrative tasks.

I then reinforced the team by adding four exceptionally talented training officers. Already experienced in general coaching, I trained them in modern techniques particular to child trafficking cases, which they eventually taught to more than 400 officers in the provinces and capital.

Adapting a verse from *Le Cid* by Corneille, "We were hardly a dozen to embark, but with swift support, grew to four hundred as we reached the port[9]."

But to reach the port and attain our goals, we first had to spend countless hours in meetings, training sessions and trips back and forth across the country to establish a complete and qualified national department devoted exclusively to fighting child sexual abuse and trafficking.

Would we have been able to launch it immediately and effectively by simply transferring surplus bureaucrats from other offices to ours? No, because this police specialization requires specific skills and qualities. You don't interview a child victim of sexual abuse the same way you interview an adult victim of robbery or fraud. And interrogating a rapist differs from interrogating a thief. The approach, the setting, the strategy, the questions you ask are different.

To collect the statement of a sexually abused or exploited child and understand it well enough to transcribe requires a capacity for listening and questioning that had to be taught to our officers. As I had limited experience with this branch of police work, an Australian police expert in the protection of minors helped us write a manual that would become our bible on the subject.

In criminal cases not involving children, surveillance, searches, crime scene analysis and interrogating suspects and witnesses is second nature to an experienced investigator, but to question a suffering child is more delicate. In Cambodia up to that time, child victims were rarely brought forward to the authorities or identified. Crimes of incest were hidden not only by the families, and even if some members were willing to seek help, they did not know whom to address. Police were not trained to look for or recognize this kind of abuse or to investigate these cases. The few children who were brought forward were questioned without any precaution or preparation, often in the presence of unreliable witnesses, and sometimes even in the presence of their aggressors. So, when it came time to go before a judge, the case might be dismissed for lack of solid evidence. Even social workers were poorly qualified – they didn't know the law or what evidence would stand up in court. The child's statements, at times mere babblings, were taken by an officer who was usually more skeptical than receptive, feet up on a desk piled with papers, coffee cups, an ashtray full of cigarette butts and maybe a machine gun or two propped up in the corner.

Our team had to wait patiently for enough funding for a special child-friendly interview room to be built where we could properly receive children, where they would be treated with tact and kindness, like the victims of profound trauma that they were, rather than like liars or worthless kids "who were asking for it." The child's testimony could be much more easily drawn-out in a "safe place."

Before our unit could be considered fully operational, we had to devote a lot of time to creating standardized documents our investigators could use to record complaints, evidence and witness statements. We also needed standardized forms for reports from technical and computer experts, and for the results of examinations and medical analyses from doctors legally appointed by the Ministry of Justice.

In affairs of this nature, where suspects often try to put the victim's statement into question, medical analyses are a crucial element. They provide solid evidence of a criminal act a child cannot or does not want to put into words. We had to make an astounding number of trips back and forth between our group and the ministries of justice and health to produce the final documents, approved by all, that would hold authority as medical proof over every procedure.

Building this administrative, judicial and pedagogical structure took many long months of work and had to be rounded out in a piecemeal fashion over the years. But it was indispensable if we were to succeed in getting prison time for guilty defendants that we brought in. It would have been easier if we could have simply reproduced standard procedures, forms, tools and techniques used in other parts of the world to produce documentary evidence. But they had to be adapted to Cambodia's legal and social environment, and to the local police culture – especially to our means on the ground. Even getting a series of good photos of a crime scene was a challenge. And procedures to perform DNA tests were of no use when there was no lab to analyze the samples. But all that would come later thanks to international aid.

Finally, I recruited our police officers, first in Phnom Penh, then in the provinces. My goal was to build a first-rate special unit. A typical investigator, paid a pittance and installed in a poorly equipped office, reimbursed for nothing but gas for his or her motorcycle while on the job, would never be up to our demands. The donors made sure we had what we needed to motivate our future troops financially, but to avoid having an army of freeloaders on the payroll I had to choose my team members carefully.

The IOs also donated money for our technical needs, like computers and cameras, and for our travel, lodging, meals and other costs of investigations. Everything was taken care of. But even with all these assets – the support of the hierarchy, the financial means – I was still conscious of the risks I was running. On terrain so chaotic, even dangerous, as that of sexual aggression against children, where it was rare to catch a criminal in the act or find material evidence, where the pressure on rank-and-file officers can be overwhelming if the accused is a stranger or a Cambodian close to the circles of power, I knew that we could not win every case or be impervious to manipulations that could lead to miscarriages of justice. Our benefactors were well aware of all this.

To my knowledge, this was UNICEF's first foray into the domain of criminal investigation, and although I was its paid consultant, my office would be in the Ministry of the Interior rather than in UNICEF headquarters. This physical distance would help protect UNICEF from getting embroiled in controversy or squabbles. I was also instructed to remain as discreet as possible in carrying on my work, to stay in the background when dealing with them or as their representatives, with suggestions, advice, and training, and make no "official" decisions. But in reality, this proved impossible, and for the Project to succeed, I had to take the initiative. It was like walking a tightrope. I remained in the background, advising the highest-level decision-makers, who gave the official orders, and then I joined the teams to physically carry out the orders. My advice translated into action.

Along with UNICEF and World Vision, several other major donors had committed to the Project, such as the International Organization for Migration (IOM), the United Nations Office of the High Commissioner for Human Rights. There were also several smaller NGOs involved, like Save the Children, Terre des Hommes and the Kamonohashi Project. But because the Project fell outside their usual expertise, they were a bit like generals without an army, so part of my role entailed collaborating with the local authorities to make sure the team I chose ensured the Project's success. This called for the greatest care when I picked the men and women to bear our service's insignia, and that meant taking the time to do it right.

After four years in police and judicial cooperation work at the French Embassy in Phnom Penh, I knew the Cambodian police force inside and out, from street cops on a miserable salary who got to work tired and dusty, two or three astride one moped, to the highest-ranking officers whose luxurious villas hinted at supplemental pay, illicit or not. Rank could be bought, and buyers recouped their investment by preying on anyone not working for or protected by the police. For example, a traffic officer rounded out his salary by pocketing fines for minor infractions like driving with the headlights on during the day or touching the white line at an intersection. Or worse: an officer collected money by providing "protection" to the countless brothels around the country.

This kind of corruption was just one of the challenges our Project had to overcome. We also had to navigate the intricacies of the "clan," the ancestral system of patronage in Cambodia, which had existed through the ages, through all political regimes, sometimes in a Mafia-like form. Everyone belonged to a clan, no matter their standing in the hierarchy, and it was the clan that helped them survive and protected them when necessary. When I first came to Cambodia and ran training sessions for criminal investigators, I insisted police officers must treat all citizens the same. But I knew that their family or clan's interests would indubitably come before those of a citizen unknown to them. That didn't prevent me from constantly returning to the subject, especially when emphasizing the difference between a felony and a misdemeanor in the order of priorities.

"If a rich businessman rushes out of his store screaming that someone stole a thousand dollars from his cash register, and demands you arrest or even kill the thief, you can't bow to his wishes," I would explain to them. "That theft is a misdemeanor, not an assassination. You report the complaint and launch an investigation, and that's all. If a prostitute is murdered on the same day as this theft, you must first fully investigate the murder, because that's a felony. Even if the victim was a poor girl, 'insignificant' compared to the rich businessman waiting in the hallway."

I drummed that scale of priorities into my officers, examining it from every angle. It probably seems obvious to people living in a developed country that a police officer would respect these priorities. But with those Cambodian police officers, it was necessary to teach priority between rich and poor, misdemeanor and felony. But I was no dupe. How much could the businessman pull out of his pocket if the cop found his money and the thief? And the injured or dead prostitute – how much could she bribe them with? Corruption existed and there was no way around it. That was how a lot of the police units funded their work, and I accepted that as a given; nevertheless, we were able to make improvements to that system.

Not all the ranking officers behaved the same way toward bribes or "rewards" that rich litigants offered them; for example, to release one of their hooligans who had been arrested under the influence of drugs or alcohol, or for locating their child who had been kidnapped and held for ransom (a common form of banditry in the 90s).

I divided these officers into three categories. First, the man of integrity. The police chief who refused any and all bribes – money or favors like releasing a friend. As a result, he was poor. His men were too and came to work only on paydays because to make ends meet, they had to work other jobs: guardian, bodyguard, moto-taxi driver. Understandably, the results of this kind of police chief's unit were non-existent.

And then we had the opposite type, all too common: the police chief who took every kind of bribe, all the dirty money, raking in whatever he could get without redistributing a dime to his men or improving their work conditions. Here again, the police didn't do much work, and their investigations fizzled out for lack of motivation or resources, like gas for their motorcycles.

The third category suited me better: the chief who accepted the envelopes but only to finance his men's work and buy the equipment they needed. Taxes did not exist then, so it was hard for the government to pay decent wages. This seemed reasonable to me in light of the local context – such "gifts" could be considered a sort of tax on the rich. Unless of course the "financing" was meant to have the unit sweep a case under the rug, or release a criminal, or accuse an innocent person of a crime.

Corruption did not end with the police; it flourished among judges and prosecutors as well. No matter how professional and ethical the work of our future units would be, the risk of a bribed magistrate throwing out our cases remained. That was one of the inherent risks I had weighed before setting up the Project. The important thing, in the beginning, was not to always win, but to win more and more often until our department was fully integrated and recognized as a legitimate force within the national police organization and the entire population.

By dint of bringing in the most dynamic and motivated workers I could find during my travels, and subjugating them to intensive training sessions, we slowly but surely strengthened our special units. My trips to the provinces were unforgettable, not just the training, often held in barracks without air conditioning, where the temperature could climb over 100 degrees, but because of the disastrous state of the roads we had to travel, potholed and dusty in the dry season, inches deep in slimy mud during the rainy season.

Managing our work travel was not to be taken lightly, considering our ambition to form a national program. Dealing with the material conditions of our missions, as secondary as that may seem, was essential if we were to respect the schedule that had been fixed. One of those conditions was adhering to regulations like the one that strictly banned cars bearing the UNICEF logo from circulating at night. That meant around six in the evening. This was a security measure, but many times it landed us in dicey situations, especially in the rainy season.

One day we took off a bit late from Banteay Meanchey heading to Siem Reap, a distance of 80 miles. We had to arrive the next morning without fail, because another mission had been painstakingly arranged, but floods carried off a bridge on our road in the middle of the countryside. Night was about to fall, and we had to find another way to cross or be doomed to sleeping in our car, a rustic Nissan Patrol, about as comfortable as a horse-cart.

Some people from a nearby village suddenly appeared out of the gloom, probably out of curiosity. After consultations with our driver, they lashed together a good dozen or so empty oil drums and some planks salvaged from the broken bridge. With this improbable raft, we could cross the forty or fifty feet separating us from the other bank. As I stood there imagining our car swept off by the river, about twenty of these strapping fellows slid the Nissan down onto the improvised raft, pushed it across and hauled it out on the other side.

None of the project leaders had thought to include an extra few hours in the work schedules for misadventures like that. I should have known better. These setbacks arose continually, part and parcel of the difficulties we had to overcome when we hit the road. Nevertheless, over the course of three years and hundreds of meetings, case studies, training sessions – all the grinding groundwork – our department developed its skilled police force until we were 150 strong within the Ministry and over 400 across the country. We established satellite units in each of the six provinces judged as "higher risk" because they are on the borders of Laos, Vietnam or Thailand or because they are more populous: Phnom Penh, Battambang, Banteay Meanchey, Siem Reap, Sihanoukville and Kandal. Once these satellite units were up and running, our activities spread to every part of the country.

Laying the groundwork was indispensable, but it took a while – we wanted it to be done right – and this put me into an awkward situation with the donors. I had promised to send child molesters to jail, and they saw little movement on that front. To satisfy their impatience and provide us a valuable tool to detect abuse cases, on October 15, 2000, we launched a hotline for victims or witnesses of child sexual abuse.

From that day forward, the hotline mobilized four police officers twenty-four hours a day, and we immediately started extricating young girls from houses of prostitution. Like the 17-year-old who was kidnapped, drugged, then sold to a "massage parlor" in Sihanoukville. A textbook case. Her sister called the hotline to alert the police, who freed her and arrested the pimp.

The hotline was the first public manifestation of our efforts and would be the first link in a chain that grew from thirty cases in 2000 to over 700 in 2005 alone. There was work to do: about a third of the approximately 15,000 sex workers in Cambodia were children from 12 to 17 years old, and half of them had become prostitutes only because they were forced to.

Cambodian people usually avoided to their local police for many reasons: lack of trust, not knowing a cop to ask for by name, or even blocking them at the door, so a few of the local NGOs, in their initial doubts, tested us by referring cases to us that only they knew about. When they realized we weren't dismissing their cases offhand, they no longer hesitated. That was when I knew this Project and its specialized service was on the right road.

Albert Camus wrote, "It is not rebellion itself which is noble but the demands it makes upon us." In other words, outrage incites us to revolt, and no matter how difficult, to put things into motion to bring justice to the wronged. In that sense, I declared myself an outraged man. As a long-time police officer, I was outraged that crimes against children were still being left unpunished, so I helped put things into motion to change that. That is where nobility in the true sense of the word comes in – acting on your moral principles, drawing on your courage, being willing to make sacrifices to change the status quo. In my personal life, I made many sacrifices, living far away from my children for two years, three, up to six years at a time, especially when I made the difficult decision to go back to Cambodia for this new, complex, even dangerous mission. And it would keep me away for ten years.

One of my goals was to transmit my sense of outrage to my fellow officers, who also pushed for justice, often in highly hostile environments. Their show of true nobility and our successful results shows how wrong it is to cry "impossible" before trying.

Another great author, Victor Hugo, wrote in *Les Misérables* that revolutions spring not from accident, but from necessity. And when there are children suffering abuse and exploitation, it is necessary to act, to revolt against the trampling of these "little flowers." Street children and little girls from poor families, rotting in brothels that became their prisons – over the course of ten years, we encountered hundreds of these abused children and saw firsthand the misery they faced.

In the pages that follow, you will meet a few of them. Their individual stories speak for all the rest.

II - The Ogre of Sihanoukville

I was still busy setting up the Project when our team was assigned a case remarkable for its complexity. Besides being our unit's "baptism in fire," it was the case that left me feeling the most bitter, for even though we had plenty of hard evidence and numerous witness statements, we failed to put the suspect behind bars. However, we learned what and what not to do from then on.

Two boys were found one day wandering the streets of Phnom Penh, their testicles bound in locks. Social workers from the NGO Mith Samlanh/Friends brought them to their facility, where a doctor examined them and removed their painful bindings. Photos presented to the courts would attest to this procedure. According to their statements, the boys came from Sihanoukville [10] after running away from the house of a man who engaged in indecent acts with them. This Frenchman, Pierre Guideno, had been suspected of pedophilia a few years earlier in Cambodia, and he was back. The NGO directors learned from the two boys that about a dozen youths, some of them under 15 years old, lived on the man's property, a recreation center with a pool and go-kart tracks. They said the man engaged in all kinds of sexual acts with them. One of the boys said he had been drugged and raped. Like some of the others, he had gone to the center after an "adopted son" of the man had approached him on the street in Phnom Penh. Posing as a generous benefactor, the man offered a roof, food, schooling, work and a few dollars to poor kids. Other boys had come from impoverished families of Sihanoukville, for whom the free admission of their child to that establishment represented a boon.

The human rights organizations LICADHO (Cambodian League for the Promotion and Defense of Human Rights) and One House put the center under surveillance and discovered its true nature. The boys wore no clothes or only those made of see-through fabrics; men were seen entering alone and leaving with a boy. Neighbors knew the owner had excessive, if not harmful authority over these children, to the point of tormenting them by putting a lock on their privates, and his sexual practices fed the local gossip.

Enlarging their field of research, the two NGOs discovered Guideno's website promoting a sadomasochistic homosexual club being set up in Sihanoukville, for which he was seeking investors. The affair now became international and led the NGOs to call on the national police. Were we on the trail of an international pedophile ring? Were Cambodian children enduring sexual abuse and torture to satisfy the fantasies of rich Western perverts?

On reviewing the file, I saw evidence that the information gathered by the NGOs justified digging deeper into the hidden side of this so-called "go-kart club."

I was aware NGOs sometimes tended to focus on affairs involving minors, to attract the attention of donors. Cambodia has one of the world's highest concentrations of NGOs, so donors have a lot of choices. The struggle against sex tourism and pedophilia targeting children in poor countries being a major subject for IO intervention, it was natural that these NGOs focus on it to generate funds to develop their activities.

There was no hesitation on my part. The project I was piloting targeted this kind of crime, and along with the national police, we had a duty to seek justice for the victims and punishment for the guilty party or parties. We weren't yet fully equipped in human and technical resources to investigate and bring the man to trial, but we would do the best we could.

The case officially taken up, our barely tested unit started interviewing the boys and their families, most of whom assured us they'd only just discovered what their children had been through.

A new finding then increased the evidence against the suspect when a woman stated her son had been locked up almost an entire day in a container placed under the house. The reason given her is that he'd been accused of stealing a chicken from the center's courtyard. She told the police the owner of the center freed her son only after she gave him 20,000 riels (5 dollars in 2022) for the "lesson" he'd given the boy. This act of sequestration, added to the locks, convinced us it was high time to handcuff this bizarre, apparently evil man.

A search was organized, all the details of which I covered beforehand with the Sihanoukville police. I still see myself in front of the suspect's house discussing with the prosecutor how important it was to treat this case with the greatest rigor, to show the world that Cambodia was resolved to punish crimes against children. While talking to the magistrate, I observed Guideno. In his forties, well-dressed, even stylish, with a light beard setting off an open face, he presented himself as a well-educated man born in easy circumstances. He seemed relaxed – yes, relaxed – even though he knew an indictment for serious crimes would follow this search. He protested vehemently against us confiscating his computer, saying he needed it for his work, that it belonged to him, but for all that, he never lost his calm. Our search allowed us to seize cameras, computer equipment, photos of naked children, pornographic videos of a pedophile nature and a handgun. All throughout this, he revealed snatches of what his line of defense would be and how it would contribute to bog down the case in a mishmash of trivial considerations unlikely to contribute to the court's serenity.

The photos of nude children? "Well, it's very hot here, isn't it?"

A child unlawfully confined? "Who's never punished a kid who's been naughty by setting him in a corner?"

Or "I do a lot more for children than those NGOs! They're jealous and that's why they'll accuse me of anything to try to harm me." And "Children will say any old thing, and their families, the NGOs, the media, or the police will push them to do just that."

He didn't shout or panic. He maintained the calm and intelligent composure of a good man, friendly and likeable, the perfect demeanor to persuade a judge hesitant to commit to a potentially awkward path.

The day after the search, the Sihanoukville prosecutor ordered Guideno to be detained temporarily, and opened a preliminary investigation for lewd acts, possession of a weapon and unlawful confinement. Strangely enough, he did not bring charges of rape and lewd acts with minors, more severely punished than the others.

Far from being a benefactor to children, the material evidence showed beyond a doubt that this was a man sexually attracted exclusively to children, that he used his go-kart club to lure them in, and then he abused them. Older boys who no longer interested him sexually became "adopted sons" and served to scout out new young boys. This evidence and the children's statements should have brought a heavy sentence down, seeing the gravity of the charges against him.

But powerful opposing winds sprang up to sweep justice in another direction entirely. His family back in France, respectable and highly placed, used their influence to get the Ministry of Foreign Affairs to intervene and extricate their descendant from his mess. They swore by all the gods that their son Pierre was a marvellous young man, good and full of charity, and they gave the Foreign Affairs Minister a cast-iron line of defense: he risked dying in his Cambodian prison because he'd undergone a heart transplant a few years earlier. You had to let him out of there; it was a question of life or death! Meaning, "What do those stupid, poorly raised kids matter when the life of a worthy Frenchman is in danger?"

Pressured by their superiors, the French Embassy in Cambodia started working behind the scenes in favor of their imprisoned fellow citizen. In a letter to the Sihanoukville prosecutor, one of the diplomats took off the kid gloves, writing that his compatriot was the victim of a cabal, and if he died in prison, it would be our fault. They enlisted other help too. Some very powerful people in Cambodia – intimates of the royal family and high-placed businessmen – who of course remained in the shadows, also pleaded the prosecutor for his release.

This pressure did not result in his immediate release, but it increased tensions in the local courts. At that time, an obscure magistrate in the provinces was of little importance compared to the grand personages in Phnom Penh, and who wants on their back the embassy of one of the most influential countries in Cambodia at that time?

The French embassy approached me, too, to request we drop the case. My team played an important role in that affair – the local police had confided to us the analyses of physical evidence and the contents of the hard disks that were seized – and we were doing our best to help our colleagues in the prosecutor's office and justice department firm up the case.

I had to grit my teeth at the wheedling of my long-time embassy friend, a security attaché. "What a bore for you, this business of a little weenie-touching! Why ruin your retirement hassling with this nonsense, when you've had a career in real crime cases? And then, are you sure you're not being had by these stupid NGOs?"

Too many times have I heard this kind of denigrating remark from old colleagues, about how working to protect children was somehow a step down for me, career-wise. In the French police, the juvenile crime unit had long been considered low on the rungs, where cops were reduced practically to the role of social assistants. On one hand were the prestigious units, the "ballsy" ones like narcotics, counterterrorism or homicide – and on the other, the juvenile units dealing with prosecution instructions. Nothing worthwhile to a "real cop." I have to admit I shared the same view while working in France, but it swiftly changed after witnessing how the children in Cambodia suffered. Thanks to several international agreements, this haughty view of child protection units is no longer the norm, and police everywhere realize the importance of protecting children from abuse and trafficking.

Bu to those who maintain the old prejudice, I repeat what I told Cambodian colleagues who continued to doubt it was a priority: "What is the most precious thing in your family – your car or your children? Your children of course. So, protecting them is top priority, and because you're a police officer, protecting other people's children should be your priority, too."

The Embassy did not get what it wanted. I refused to drop the case. I understood why they tried; after all, one of an embassy's functions is to offer consular protection to their citizens and make sure those who are imprisoned are treated correctly and given medical care if necessary. Plus, having a

Frenchman implicated in a pedocriminal case gave a very poor impression of France. Even so, no diplomat should ever try to minimize the allegations against a suspect or belittle those of us trying to protect children by getting a pedophile off the streets.

They were not the only ones to spread the idea this case was nothing but "weenie-touching on the playground." Other people tried to credit the so-called recreation center for lifting those children out of abject poverty without causing them too much suffering. Yet more voices chimed in, claiming the children had reached puberty, and benefited from finding interest and even pleasure in discovering their sexuality with an adult.

It's not inconceivable they found pleasure in it. And for street children, orphans and abandoned kids in Phnom Penh, their precarious social environment certainly was terrible. Children had a hard time. They had to adapt to violence, drugs and beggary, schooling was rare, and work was hard to find. There was no comfort, no future on the streets or in destitute homes, so the perspective of a peaceful haven could attract them, even if the price was giving their body for sexual services.

But we were the police, and these considerations did not enter the picture. The law forbids all acts of a sexual nature, with or without penetration, between adults and minors under fifteen, the legislature having determined a child is incapable of freely consenting to sexual relations with an adult. It follows that an adult cannot shirk responsibility by claiming the child had consented. Period.

But Pierre Guideno and his lawyers twisted this interpretation of the law to argue that because a child is indeed "irresponsible," the judge should dismiss the case as an orchestrated attack by certain NGOs who made these children say one thing because they had money (donations) riding on it, and then its exact opposite. One of the young boys whose testicles were held in a lock had recanted, saying he'd been manipulated by the members of the NGO that helped him. And although the other children and their families all concurred in the accusations, their solidarity fractured during the investigation period, so much so that the number of plaintiffs changed, and certain witness statements were retracted.

Were they bribed by the defendant's relatives, as the prosecution claimed? No one will ever know.

In the end, nothing beats material evidence. Children could very well lie, invent acts or modify the nature of those acts to hurt the person they're accusing, or they might lie to protect them. They shouldn't be left alone to face people who disparage their truthfulness, threaten them or entice them with compensation. But we do have to listen to them, because when a case comes down to "his word against my word," especially that of a child's against an adult's, justice is not blind, but nearly so.

That's why, lacking ironclad material evidence, the examining prosecutor went easy on the well-born Frenchman, abandoning the charge of rape and reassigning the charge of confinement to one of his "adopted sons." Only the accusations of possession of an illegal firearm and lewd behavior – but not toward a minor – were retained. The first charges were dismissed for lack of evidence. And yet six children testified their former "benefactor" had sexually abused them. All for nothing. At the end of the hearing, Guiden was released on bail and forbidden to leave the country.

Obviously, the case cried out for appeal. The attorney-general requested a detailed report of the proofs in hand, and after I gave it to him, he rejected the sentence. But oddly enough, he ordered the case retried in Sihanoukville rather than appealing it in Phnom Penh, and a new trial was held a few months later. I was hoping it would correct the outcome of the first even though some witnesses retracted their statements, which bid no good. But the case was still a weighty one at the second trial. Claims, testimonies, photos and videos, the website featuring sexually abused children captioned as first sexual experiences. The videos did not show the defendant himself but brought out elements about his sexual orientation and his preference for young adolescents.

But can justice be serenely served when direct and indirect pressure has for months been put on it to minimize the gravity of a case? Once again, the charge of lewd behavior fell through the cracks and the confinement accusation landed on the "adopted son," who was condemned to three years in prison, in absentia; he had disappeared, of course.

Our perpetrator ended up sentenced to six months in prison for the pistol we found while searching his property. It had turned out to be a blank-firing gun, but it was illegal all the same.

"Mama, I'm free! It went well. I'll tell you the whole story," he announced to his mother, all smiles, in an ostentatious show before a crowd of journalists as he exited the courthouse, while a few of his protégés jeered nastily at some of the children who had made the claims.

Disgusted, the NGOs started a civil action by filing a complaint against the man in France. But he died before he could reappear in a court of justice.

From the police and judiciary's point of view, this case was a fiasco. But there were a few good results, the most important being, in my opinion, that as soon as he was exposed by the NGOs, the fake Good Samaritan could no longer harm children. Plus, the case served to teach us several things. My new colleagues, novices in dealing with sexual crimes of this nature, learned the importance of conducting a thorough search-and-seizure, of analyzing computer data, of how fragile witness statements can be and of protecting them and their cases against the interests and pressures of influential parties.

This case reinforced my belief of how worthy our mission was. Cambodia needed to correct its image of a country where crimes against children go unpunished, and the media coverage of this affair helped by warning off pedophile predators from around the world who saw this little nation as a chosen land. As disappointing as the case's judicial outcome was, it signaled that Cambodia would no longer shut its eyes to their criminal activities.

III - The Pedophile of the Woods

"Hey, I know him! That's Tum. He's from Takeo."

The shoeshine boy was pointing at a photo on the front page of my newspaper. A naked child about 10 years old stood with his hands over his crotch next to three other boys, also nude, and a naked man of about thirty, who was squatting on the ground gazing into space. The police had just arrested the man, a foreigner, for having sexual relations with minors. They'd caught him in the act with these children in a bamboo forest on the Tonlé Sap, a river fed by a large lake bearing the same name. The Tonlé Sap flows into the Mekong, converging at "Quatre Bras," (four arms) in Phnom Penh, with its central point in front of the Royal Palace, "as the gods willed."

That morning, my colleague Heng Long and I had left our shoes with the shoeshine boy while we ate *kuy teav*, the traditional Cambodian soup of rice noodles, pork bouillon and garnishes, on a riverside café terrace. Since my arrival in Cambodia, I had gotten into the habit of cheerfully greeting these children wandering about the restaurant terraces trying to earn a bit of money. Each of them carried a wooden box full of brushes, wax, and rags, hanging from their necks on a strap, and for 500 riels[11], they transformed your scuffed and dusty shoes to smooth and glossy in just minutes. I had refused the services of the first shoeshine boy who approached me, but gave him some money anyway, not wanting to seem like a rancorous old colonist. Heng Long told me that was a mistake.

"*Lok kru*[12]," he said. "These kids are 10 to 15 years old, and most of them come to Phnom Penh to escape famine in areas devastated by drought or flooding. But when they arrive, without any family, they're often reduced to begging. Having a job improves their social status. Instead of being beggars, they're workers, and more respected."

He turned to the shoeshine boy. "So, you know the boy in the photo? Let's hear all about him, but first tell me your name and where you come from."

"My name's Sipho and I'm from Battambang. I'm 13. My parents and two younger sisters live in a village. My dad's a farm worker, and mama makes little cakes she sells at the school and the pagoda. I couldn't earn anything to help them, so I left with two friends from my village. One went to a landfill to work with the ragpickers, and the other stayed with me a few weeks then left for his uncle's place in Kampong Chhnang to fish in the Grand Lac."

"You stayed here alone?"

"I made friends from Kampong Cham, Kratie, and other provinces. We sleep together under the carport of a shophouse[13]. It's in an alley by the central Market. At first, we begged, but we earned only a few thousand riels a days, so we decided to buy a shoeshine kit. We all put in a little money and bought one, then two, and now we each have one. At night, the owner of the shophouse where we sleep guards our boxes so they don't get stolen. We always stay together to defend ourselves. We wash when it rains, but after the rainy season the house owner sometimes leaves us water to wash up a bit. For going to the bathroom, we figure out ways. We're kind of like lost dogs."

Sipho buried his embarrassment by laughing.

"Where are your friends?"

"All four of us work this street, as there are plenty of cafés and two restaurants with terraces. We each earn from 5,000 to 7,000 riels a day, a lot more than from begging. But there's another team over on the Sisowath quai, and sometimes they come and try to take our customers from us. Then we have a big argument, and sometimes we fight."

"What about going to school?"

"I can't attend now, but I want to go again when it's back in session. I'll work in the evenings."

"Now tell me about this boy Tum."

"There were six of us shoeshine boys at first, but Tum and Thy went off with some Vietnamese lady who promised them 5 dollars a day if they were good. But I think what they're doing is bad."

"What are they doing?"

The kid smiled and said, "They have sex, *boum boum*,[14] with men in their *kdeth*[15] and mouth. They live by Svay Pak. It's kind of far from Phnom Penh, but they visit us sometimes. They've got nicer clothes now, but they're always being watched, and I know they earn only 2 or 3 dollars with each client. Plus, their bosses hit them. So do mean tourists when they don't want to do things. But Tum told me he prefers that kind of work anyway, because he can see more places and earn more, and some customers act nice. They give him presents. He said he gets pleasure from doing what he does. But I'd never do that. I think of my parents – they'd be so unhappy! And I hope to have a girlfriend one day when I'm grown up."

My colleague Heng Long was a good man, and this hard-working boy and his story had touched a chord – his childhood in a workcamp under the Khmer Rouge had been even worse.

"You tell your friends not to do what Tum does," he said. "Tell them a police officer told you, one whose job it is to protect you kids from men like the one in the photo."

He fished in his pocket and took out some money.

"Here's a thousand riels for your work. Our shoes look great, thank you. We'll come back again one of these days and I'll bring you a workbook. Now be careful out there."

The photo of the boy Tum we had been talking about was on the newspaper's front page because two days earlier, the Phnom Penh court had condemned this European tourist known as the "Pedophile of the Woods" to ten years in prison for lewd acts with boys aged 11 to 14.

The crime had occurred the previous year, in June 2001, and our team had handled the case, a typical example of a form of pedophilia targeting street children, whom sex tourists sought out because they were vulnerable, destitute, and without protection.

I still remember it twenty years later, because it was the unit's first case of "flagrante delicto."

Local police had been notified of a suspicious stranger accompanied by some children. They were found about a hundred feet from a river, by a house on pilings perched above the reeds covering the riverbanks. It was the intermediate season, when brief but heavy monsoon rains refreshed the end of each day.

When the police accosted the man, an Italian named Mario Cozzino, naked and in that highly compromising position recorded in the news photo, he did not react; he seemed dazed at seeing four officers glaring at him. They took photos and localized the crime scene, gathered the evidence – video and still cameras, gels, condoms – and brought the man to the commissary, wearing clothes and handcuffs by that point. They then transferred him to our new child protection unit in Phnom Penh, whose rooms still smelled of paint, and locked him up. They marshalled the boys into a separate interview room we had finally been able to set up. This was a child-friendly spot arranged to put them at ease, unlike the old interview room, grimy and cluttered with files and half a dozen Kalashnikovs, where on-duty cops wandered in and out without an inkling of what was going on.

Normally, the police would first search for the parents, but these kids said they had none, or they lived far away. In this situation, the unit would call in a social services worker or one of the NGOs to help the victims and locate attorneys for them.

Our trained investigator got ready to question the four boys one by one, her goal being to gather as much information as possible: identity, family, history, where they lived, their daily lives. We also wanted to find out who introduced them to the perpetrator, and the exact nature of the acts he had committed. Touching, penetration, money received or promised – all had to be recorded in maximum detail.

She began by offering water, then, speaking calmly to put them at ease, she asked how they ended up in Phnom Penh. She then oriented the discussion toward getting each child to confide in her about his other "clients" or men his boss asked him to meet for sex. It was important to identify their bosses and any other accomplices, information that was difficult to extract. The boys feared their bosses would retaliate if they talked and they didn't know what would happen to them later, without our promises of protection.

We were all familiar with Tum's course, which was similar to that of the other boys. An orphan, Tum had gotten along by begging before he met Madam X, the tenant of a Kieng Svay bar located between two brothels. Then came his first client, and along with that, new tennis shoes, a "cool" Nike T-shirt and a lot of pain when he went caca. Then came more clients, Asians and Westerners, at least four or five a week. Like the other boys, Tum eventually got used to it, and they all received condoms and a tube of gel or Vaseline.

Madam X grumbled whenever he came back without any money, Tum told the investigator. "She often pointed us to a client, but sometimes we had to find them ourselves by talking to men on the bar terraces. The guy you arrested wanted all four of us to play naked in the reeds on the riverbank. At first, he watched us, then he asked us to touch his genitals and caress him, like a game. Then he told my buddy Ho to masturbate him slowly, and he did *boum-boum* with him. That's when we heard noise and shouting, and I saw the police arrive. We couldn't run away. Ho got up and the tourist sat down in the grass, completely naked."

The investigator patiently logged her questions and the boys' answers on a laptop, following a template. Ours was one of the rare Phnom Penh police units with computers and standardized forms we had created for procedural acts. This made it easier to collect and record information, and allowed our investigators to concentrate on listening to a child in a relaxed situation, more favorable for confidences.

Before the LEASETC Project and the creation of our unit, the police would have considered this 12-year-old boy not as a victim but as a good-for-nothing. They would have made him cry by reproaching him for hanging around bad men and made him feel dirty by accusing him of taking part in degrading acts. They would have chided him, saying he should have run away and denounced the offender to the police, and worst of all, they would have told him he'd brought shame to his parents and his whole village.

But now, our questioners were trained, and they got better results by creating an ambiance of psychological comfort, instead of adding more suffering and stress to the child's trauma. They reassured them by saying we were there to protect them. Only by winning their trust could our investigators collect all the important details about these pedophiles' crimes. Victims' statements are vital, for they add weight to any eventual outside declarations and to the physical evidence found at the scene of the crime or during a search under warrant; it all adds up to a body of evidence that can later be used not just in court, but in interrogating the suspect or suspects.

During the five or so hours it took to examine these boys, night had fallen over Phnom Penh. Cozzino had used the time to reflect and compose a new character for himself. The investigating officer had questioned him briefly in the chief's office, notifying him he was under arrest and would be held, but he'd waited to collect as many elements as possible before thoroughly interrogating him, as was customary. When that time came, Cozzino seemed more assured of himself, now he was dressed in a classy shirt and tailored shorts. Tall, thin, thirtyish, with black hair that was still nicely groomed despite the circumstances, his appearance belied the mistaken belief that all pedophiles are old, chubby, and repulsive.

He admitted to having been found naked in the presence of four naked boys.

"But I didn't harm them," he said. "They're the ones who approached me when I was having a drink in a bar in Svay Pak. The owner, who I don't know, said to take a walk with them, that they would be nice with me. She told me to give her twenty dollars first, for all four of them, saying she had to feed them. I made a deal and gave her sixteen. They told me they would show me the river and took me along an overgrown path past a fisherman's hut. I took off my clothes because it was hot, and I thought we would take a swim. They're the ones who encouraged me to have sexual relations, and I accepted because I'm attracted to young boys. They're street kids who've been prostituting themselves for a long time, and I'm not the one who perverted them, as you accuse me of doing."

The commandant lost his temper.

"Those are poor children, only eleven to fourteen years old!" he said. "If they propositioned you, you should have refused and told them you don't go with children. You should have told them they were on a dangerous path. I don't have time to waste with your justifications – let's get back to the facts."

He pointed at a photo. "You admit to having sexual relations with little Ho here, a 12-year-old boy, and having asked the others to touch you and masturbate you?"

"Yes, but I can explain—"

"We'll see about that tomorrow! You will remain in custody. I'm informing the prosecutor, then we'll contact your embassy. You have the right to a lawyer."

In court a few weeks later, Cozzino held to the same language and defiant air towards the authorities, pointing at the witnesses with his forefinger, a very impolite gesture in Cambodia, by the way.

"Those kids wander the streets, and they'll do anything for a few dollars," he said. "So I'm not responsible for their situation."

The judge responded witheringly, "Even if these children encouraged you to have sexual relations to earn a little money, as you claim, you're an adult, a mature and sensible man, and you should have advised them to go to school and learn a real trade, not to prostitute themselves to pedophiles. On the contrary, you did not repulse their advances. You abused these young boys and insulted their human dignity."

"I don't recognize this court. I'm going to file a complaint in my own country. In any case, I'm going to appeal."

His complaints and appeals all came to nothing.

Apart from his criminal acts, it was perhaps Cozzino's animosity that earned him ten years in prison. The Phnom Penh court's exemplary sentence against the "Pedophile of the Woods" came at just the right moment to revitalize our team morale after the Sihanoukville court had shattered it by its unjustifiable clemency toward the Ogre, a supposed "go-kart club director" who got away with similar terrible acts toward mere children.

IV - Such a Sweet Professor

Until 1996, life was good for John Miller, a professor in his native land of Great Britain. He was married, with a family, and as a teacher he was appreciated by parents for his kindness toward children. Plus, he was happy because he was able to indulge, with complete confidence and tranquility, in sexual aggressions against little girls.

It lasted from 1979 to 1996. Fifteen years of pleasure and impunity for Miller, whom no one suspected of anything untoward, let alone things so infamous and perverted. He was just so sweet to the kids. But how many little girls did he abuse during all that time? No one knows exactly, but when the long-silent victims began to speak up, first one, then another, the number of *known* cases came to nineteen. Nineteen victims, nineteen lives mutilated.

When the police net began to close in, Miller decided to clear out. His destination? Cambodia. To his friends, he claimed he wanted to consecrate the rest of his life to humanitarian efforts, and Cambodia was a logical choice from that point of view, since there were so many NGOs there.

Before selecting his new homeland, it's apparent the professor did his research to find the places most advantageous to his predilection. It all pointed to this small exotic nation stuck between Thailand and Vietnam. It wasn't the Angkor temples, those grandiose monuments to the Khmer empire's former power, or Sihanoukville's fine sandy beach dotted with palms and lapped by azure waters, or the tranquil Cambodian countryside and its rice paddies that held Miller's attention at this critical moment in his life. No, what interested him was how easy it would be to settle in a country with a faltering administration, where you could wriggle out of delicate situations with a few well-placed bills, and with a high population of young children whose poverty helped make them accessible to a "hunter" like him. Cambodia seemed the perfect asylum. In 2000, it was notorious around the globe as a pedophile's paradise.

He ended up running an English school in Phnom Penh – a dream job for Miller. Back then, opening an English school was easy. Ever since Cambodia had joined the Association of Southeast Asian Nations[16], or ASEAN, the language of Shakespeare had relegated that of Molière to the background, despite the country's history as a French protectorate. Mastering English had become the magic key not only to get into college but also to get a good job, and parents with any money sent their children to an English school as a matter of course.

But aside from a handful of schools offering a serious curriculum and competent professors, most schools would employ just about anyone, as long as they came from an English-speaking country. The local authorities didn't look too closely into an instructor's teaching qualifications back then, and many of these people lacked any. They could be students on break, truck drivers, veterans, typesetters, but all became English "professors," and there were enough of them that a motley and often alcoholic expatriate community formed, where anybody could easily slide in and hide.

Being English, and by chance a real professor, Miller launched his own school without the least difficulty. He set it up in a huge wooden house based on traditional Khmer home construction. Built on pilings, with a large central hall and spacious bedrooms, these houses are designed so air circulates freely, and the rooms are protected from the sun's rays, important in a place like Phnom Penh, where it can reach 100 degrees in the shade at the height of the dry season.

Miller took in 60 students a day in groups of 10 to 20, which allowed him to support himself correctly. Soon after establishing himself in this new life as an upright professor, he started hunting again, cameras around his neck, candy in his pockets. A caricature of a pedophile. But as in England, he gained people's trust with his respectable look: neatly cut gray hair, casual clothes, big smiles, kindly glances. He cultivated his image of "doting grandpa" full of compassion, gushing at the country's fascinating charm, at the natural grace and incredible kindness of this people who had suffered so much...and going into raptures over the delicate and luminous beauty of the little girls with "bodies worthy of an Apsara[17]."

Sweetness and charm on the outside, lechery on the inside.

Miller liked to go for a walk on Sundays, especially in Takhmau, a little town in Phnom Penh's southern outskirts that hugs the banks of the Tonle Bassac, another arm of the Mekong River. Pagodas, Buddhas, parks and ponds make Takhmau an agreeable recreation spot close to the capital. Crowds of children play in the streets of the town while their parents are busy at the market or in a shop or working the land.

Young girls playing by themselves in small groups were Miller's preferred target. At times, they would wander the rice paddies after harvest to gather rice scattered over the dry ground, then went to the riverbank to cool off, where they splashed merrily, lifting their skirts so they wouldn't get wet. Miller was never far off, taking photos or videos with an innocent smile on his face.

Our special unit learned all about his strategy. He would make his first move by approaching and gesturing to them in a friendly way.

"Do you want to see the pretty pictures I took?"

"Yes!" they would shout, laughing. And four or five girls would group around the oh-so-engaging photographer.

"Hey, what's this – candies in my pocket! Why don't we play a game? You lift your skirt, then I have to take a photo before it falls back down. Then you come get a piece of candy out of my pocket. Yes, like that. Do it again – turn around."

And the game got more and more perverse.

"Show your panties! How about going swimming together, but we take off our clothes first so they won't get wet?"

Then the touching started. Finally, he would isolate the one he thought was prettiest and most naïve.

It all proceeded as in a game, with smiles and laughter.

"But I never raped any of those girls," he said later in his defense. "I watched them, and took pictures and videos of them and touched them a little bit. It's not that serious, and they found it amusing. Yes, I masturbated in front of them, but discreetly, without alarming them."

How thoughtful of you, John Miller.

He carried on his "discreet" activities several times at the riverside, then in the park, and behind the pagoda. In what was then but a large village, word gets around fast, and people began to whisper things like, "Isn't it strange how that *barang*[18] coaxes the little girls and clowns around with them?"

Very few Westerners lived in that area and those few were seen mostly in restaurants or cafés in town. They would visit the pagodas or watch the fishing boats pass along the river, but you certainly didn't see them playing with children. The local police were finally alerted about this peculiar behavior, and our unit got involved, first by sending them binoculars and a camera. After briefly questioning the witnesses who had notified the police, then the fishermen living near the river, they caught Miller on August 26, 2000, on the stairs linking the river and the pagoda. He was squatting down to film under some little girls' skirts. He tried, in vain, to throw his video camera into the river.

The chief of the child-protection bureau (part of AHTJP) and my translator Kong Sun interviewed the two girls, while I remained in the background to give advice or guide my colleagues when they stumbled, took the wrong avenue or put on too much pressure to bring out the information we needed to put this pedophile behind bars.

One of the girls was 8 years old; the other was 10. They referred to Miller as "Mr. John," and said he often came to Takhmau, that he gave them candies and sometimes 1,000 riels to let him touch them. And worse. The little girls testified their aggressor injected something into the arms of two girls in their group, rendering them unconscious. The interview brought nothing else. The chief was not yet fully trained; from misplaced modesty, she kept hesitating to get into precise detail. No medical analysis could be done either, for lack of expertise and technical resources at the time.

After getting a warrant to search Miller's home, our police officers found numerous indecent photos of young girls, pornographic films featuring children downloaded from the internet, and other films he had produced himself showing little girls in provocative outfits. They also found four new syringes, but no injectable products. Undoubtedly, there was more that could have been used as solid evidence, but the special unit was still in its infancy; its members still lacked field experience and the kind of know-how one picks up from dealing with similar cases. The objects seized proved nothing substantial against Miller: no rape, no injury, no damages. "On the contrary," he assured us during questioning. "The little girls were happy to play with me and be filmed or photographed."

Were they happy to be injected too?

"An invention made up by those children! The syringes discovered at my house are for my own use when I'm sick."

Then he started playing at being indignant, and from that to threatening us.

"I don't see the harm in all this. You should be aware that I'm a professor, and I know how to behave with children. What's more, may I remind you I hold a British passport? If you keep harassing me, I'll inform my embassy."

He nearly slipped out of our grasp. But the next day, an article appeared in the daily newspaper *Cambodge Soir* relating the first elements of the inquest. The case could no longer be kept suppressed, even if the British Embassy were to try, when the English-language press took up the report. Opinions among the townspeople were divided, and in scraps of conversation you heard,

"Scandalous behavior for a teacher," or "Why just him when there are so many others?" The case brought on a barrage of interference from every direction, even from the Ministry of the Interior, where a few officials let themselves be swayed by the perpetrator's innocent airs and apparent disinterest.

Until his judgment, Miller stuck to his original line of defense, repeating ad nauseum: "I never raped any of those girls. I looked at them, photographed and filmed them, and fondled them a little. It's not that serious and they found it amusing. I masturbated in front of them, but discreetly, without shocking them."

John Miller spent two miserable months in jail awaiting his trial, but when he appeared before the Kandal provincial court he had a wide smile plastered on his face. He thought the 5,400 dollars he'd paid to his lawyer to "take care of the affair" would lead to his immediate release. He had no desire to return to his filthy cell. For the first part of the hearing, nothing happened to trouble his smug, satisfied look. His lawyer cursorily translated the arguments being carried on in Khmer, but he seemed to consider them mere play-acting to give the trial a semblance of gravity and credibility. The longer it went on though, the more his lawyer squirmed whenever Miller looked at him questioningly.

After an hour of this strange comedy, the verdict fell: three years in prison for lewd behavior to children under 15 years old. Miller's face became livid, as if an uppercut had knocked the breath out of him. Then he exploded.

"You crooks! I paid 5,400 dollars. I was supposed to be freed today and finally recognized as innocent. That's not justice – it's highway robbery!"

He grabbed a chair and hurled it at the judge.

"You're robbers!"

The guards approached him, and he began to sob.

"I'll die if you put me back in that prison!"

Since he had arrived in Cambodia and began working, newspaper articles and his foreign friends' stories had convinced him that any problem with the police or the courts there could be "taken care of." All you needed was an intermediary, such as a lawyer. He knew dozens of foreigners had been arrested over the course of preceding years for the same kind of crime, but held only briefly, and they had come out of it just fine. He must have wondered that day, and during his entire imprisonment: "Why didn't it work for me?"

It's simple. The others had paid damages to the families and negotiated through the local police chief, for whom this kind of thing was an ideal arrangement, a win-win for both parties, as well as a "supplement" to his salary and the salaries of other authorities involved in the case.

Those other criminals may also have benefited by having their embassy intercede on their behalf. As we saw in a preceding case, embassies don't appreciate having their citizens exposed to the shame of criminal implications, which the local authorities can use against the embassy if the occasion arises. To avoid that, diplomats pull strings to try to get their compatriots freed, even pedocriminals. They object to "inhumane prison conditions" or insist "the crime was less serious in light of the local context," hinting that many Cambodian men have sex with youthful virgins and never face a court for it. This last was true, but they were smarter about it than Miller, more systematic, and they never revealed their sexual urges in public places, as he had. But now that our Project was taking on steam, these men, with their impunity in bragging about "bagging a virgin," would not get away with it much longer, as we will see later in this book.

And Miller was plain unlucky. He was arrested right when the government, pressured by the NGOs and the media, had decided to mobilize to protect children, and he faced the pugnacious Minister for Status of Women, Mu Sochua, and the Ministry of the Interior.

Miller was one of the first to serve time for a sex crime in Cambodia. If, once out of jail, he had hoped to remain there and take up his life as a teacher and stay out of the clutches of his native country, he was wrong. The United Kingdom still had him in its crosshairs. He was extradited a few months after being released, to serve the fifteen years' imprisonment the English courts had sentenced him to in absentia in 2001.

This case heralded the demise of Cambodia's reputation as being hospitable to professors of that ilk. It was partly because of you, "Mr. John." But that doesn't mean I'll be thanking you.

V - Little Flowers – Part One

Ngoc stared at the ground. As if not being able to see what was going on around her could make her invisible. As if she had committed an offense. The little girl was naked, and she sat on a miserable bed of wooden slats covered with garish cushions. She looked to be only 10 or 11 years old, as her chest was still flat.

Next to the frail child, who was as slight as a blade of grass, sat a corpulent man in his forties. He was also naked, and his hands were hiding his private parts. His astonished gaze revealed his disarray; he saw that someone was photographing the scene, irrefutable proof of his guilt.

This occurred in a wooden shanty roofed with corrugated metal, in the red-light district of Svay Pak, the famous "Kilometer 11" or K-11. This was a stretch of Route 5 that linked Phnom Penh with the northern part of the country, passing through Kampong Chhnang, a town on the Tonlé Sap estuary.

In 2002, this red-light district was booming, in plain view and in the full awareness of all. The first clients started coming in 1994. Run by pimps and *mama-san*, mainly Vietnamese nationals, the local police not only tolerated the brothels but made money on them. Between 300 and 400 prostitutes worked, or rather, were exploited in those houses of ill-repute.

Very young girls figured among those hundreds. Although clients did not openly negotiate for them, as was normal for older teens and women, the K-11 district enjoyed a national and international reputation for "fresh meat," as little girls were crudely called. The people making money from prostituting these children called them "Little Flowers," a falsely poetic name that helped wash themselves clean from moral misgivings and put the customers more at ease when breaking them in to their trade. Ngoc was one of these Little Flowers, and the corpulent man, an Italian tourist, was her first "client."

However, the police in the K-11 district had received an alert about the foreigner and they intervened, saving Ngoc from a traumatic sexual experience. Our unit was assigned the case two days later. The police report stated that the perpetrator, Antonio Rossi, had arrived in Svay Pak early in the afternoon and went to drink beer in a bar with his motorcycle-taxi driver, or *moto-dop*.

A Cambodian man about 18 years old approached him at the bar and asked if he wanted a girl, as is the usual method of hooking up clients with girls. Rossi accepted, and followed him into a nearby house, where a Vietnamese man presented him with two very young girls. Rossi refused those two. Instead, he chose an even younger girl, little Ngoc, who had been trying to hide behind the others. The three children had been living in a neighboring house for the previous month, being groomed for prostitution "on demand."

However, when the man entered the shanty and was left alone with Ngoc, a 16-year-old Vietnamese laborer noticed, and immediately called the police, who arrived about twenty minutes later and saw a naked man on the bed with Ngoc, who was naked too. The owner of the house was absent.

What happened during those 20 minutes? According to Rossi's written statement, nothing of course.

"I arrived in Phnom Penh on October 31 to spend my vacation in Cambodia and to see General S., the owner of a hotel. I spent the day of November 3 visiting the central market, which tired me out, because it was very hot. As the sauna-massage parlor at my hotel was closed in the afternoon, my *moto-dop* proposed to drive me to Svay Pak for a massage. I knew it was a dangerous place, but I agreed to go have a drink out of curiosity. Once I got there, I drank two beers at a bar and two boys approached me and asked me to follow them. I accepted, thinking it was to go to a massage parlor. I found myself in a little bedroom and they presented me with three girls. I only wanted a massage. I asked how old the girls were, but the guys didn't answer. They left with two of the girls and I stayed there with the third. I didn't know her age and I didn't intend any harm to her. It's true that when the police arrived, I was nude and the girl was too, but I hadn't done anything. I regret having gone there with my *moto-dop*."

Always the same responses. "I'm nice, I didn't do anything bad to the little girl, I didn't know she was so young..." And if they knew someone important, like General S., they always made sure to slip in their name. What followed reveals what happens only too often in this kind of case.

Ngoc contradicted Rossi during one of her first interviews. She made it clear he had chosen her from among the three girls.

"He asked me to undress, and he touched me," she muttered. "We were supposed to have sex, but the police came in."

We determined that contrary to his statements, Rossi knew he wasn't entering a massage salon, but a house of prostitution familiar to him, since he'd visited Svay Pak on an earlier trip. It was also clear he had voluntarily chosen the youngest girl, Ngoc, and could not doubt she was under fifteen, and that he'd paid five dollars to do whatever he wanted with her. The girl had not been brought into his presence without his knowing it, but because he had asked for her.

Five dollars. Five miserable dollars to crush the Little Flower Ngoc, already trampled by all the others that had brought her into his hands – that revolts me. Even more so because a few days after his arrest, the Italian managed to flee the country, benefiting most likely from the intercession of someone in a high position, and from a combination of circumstances fortuitous to Rossi.

First, the affair took place while Cambodia was hosting fifteen heads of state from the ASEAN nations, China, Japan, India, etc. All police forces were mobilized to maintain security at this event, so the child exploitation investigation was conducted hastily and poorly by the specialized office in Phnom Penh.

Then, through a blunder or intentional neglect, Rossi's passport, which had been confiscated when the police searched his hotel room, was turned in to the French embassy (at that time, Italy had no embassy in Cambodia, so the French embassy represented him) rather than being held.

Finally, after numerous interventions, probably instigated by his business associate General S., the chief of the Phnom Penh criminal investigation department received orders to release him "provisionally." It was easy for the Italian to recover his passport and disappear.

Were we going to let it slide just because the suspect had run away? Certainly not. Our goal was to arrest and lock up predators. But not only the pedophiles themselves. We also worked to pursue and condemn all accomplices to crimes of pedophilia – child traffickers, procureurs, intermediaries – and to send a clear warning to anyone who covered for them or helped them escape justice.

General Un Sokunthea said it quite succinctly: "Let these gentlemen of the police, the army, and the embassies know that by protecting a pedophile, they expose themselves to heavy backlash."

Our first act was to alert INTERPOL[19]. Any escaped criminal should fear being arrested no matter where he hides. With such a strong case, with the incontestable proof we had gathered, I trusted the Italian authorities would be highly interested, especially when we learned Antonio Rossi had already been a suspect in a similar affair. In Italy, the law allows no compromise in matters of pedophilia.

Incidentally, this brings up the problem of tracking this kind of unsavory individual, whether suspected or already condemned, and curtailing his or her freedom to travel to countries reputed to be rich "hunting grounds." Despite commitments made at international meetings, only a few countries in the world tracked their pedophile citizens and, via INTERPOL, warned the police in countries they might visit. Even in 2024, the systematic transmission of this kind of information on both national and international levels remains insufficient. As an example, France's national education department is not even informed of known pedophile behavior in teaching job candidates, an omission that shocks parents whose children could be exposed to this type of person. In the United States, regardless of background checks and obligatory registration as a sex offender, there are loopholes allowing pedophiles to continue their activities and work in schools.

With INTERPOL warned, I asked for help from Heng Peo, then deputy commissioner of the Phnom Penh municipal police charged with criminal investigations. I was on good terms with Heng, for he had been one of the top students in my 1994-1995 training sessions. He committed himself to the task without a second's hesitation. I recommended he arrest every person who had contributed to the exploitation of this young victim. The brothel owner and his brutes who sold an 11-year-old girl to a pedophile client were guilty of "aggravated procuring of a minor under fifteen years of age or aiding and abetting procuring." They had to be punished. Even the teenager who alerted the police was probably culpable, because you don't find yourself in Svay Pak at such a moment by accident. Maybe the brothel manager had swindled him of a promised reward, or he wanted to earn points for good behavior with the police. Bringing down a naïve sex tourist now and then is a small price to pay to be allowed to continue pimping for local clients wild for "Little Flowers."

The deputy commissioner assured me he would find out why the criminal had been released, what interventions he may have benefited from, what his business relations with General S. were and if the top police hierarchy bore any responsibility for his slipping out of our grasp.

Despite its frustrating ending, this case helped us take another step in improving case quality by including medical expertise. We were able to confide Ngoc to a pediatrician working in Cambodia temporarily with a non-profit agency, so clinical exams were performed that helped support accusations against all the actors in the crime, from the pedophile to the pimps.

When suspects claim they can't guess the age of their victim, or if they argue about the age by saying the boy or girl had false identity papers, we can produce X-rays of the forearm, teeth and genital organs that establish the child's age and incontestably show the difference between a child of 11 to 13 and an adult of 18, differences that are pretty obvious at first glance even without X-rays.

This clinical exam also revealed that Ngoc had been enduring anal and vaginal penetration for at least a month prior to when she was found with Rossi. She confirmed this during questioning by nodding her head or giving us summary responses: Yes. Sometimes. Often. It hurt. I cried. I had to, because my mother owed money.

Mumbled words that dropped from her mouth like so many petals painfully torn from a flower. A "Little Flower" only 11 years old.

VI - Little Flowers – Part Two

Her name was Seca, and she was 14 when we pulled her from the grip of a rich Cambodian businessman. We'll call him Poan Sarin. He had "ordered" her from a brothel owner. He planned to deflower her, then rape her as many times as he wished over the course of a few days. He indulged himself this way whenever his wife went took off on shopping trips to the designer stores in Bangkok or to visit her family in the provinces.

Poan satisfied his taste for virgins without giving a second thought to legal consequences. He had bought the title of *Oknha*[20], which gave him confidence in his immunity. Like many, Poan believed that "consuming" virgins guaranteed eternal virility and came with the added benefit of being without risk of contracting AIDS, an incorrect assumption, by the way. Poan knew of course that in stealing their virginity, the girls he raped would have difficulty finding a husband and become a dead weight to their families, and to survive, they would have few options other than entering the prostitution circuit. But he couldn't care less. He was rich and could do whatever he liked – indubitable proof he had good karma. These girls were poor, so they had bad karma. Thus spins the cycle of life for these "Sunday" Buddhists, who think if they lavish the neighborhood pagoda with gifts, they will win forgiveness for their earthly vices and guarantee happy future lives.

Seca was one of the lucky Little Flowers, as she escaped untouched. When our unit reached Poan's home, a gigantic, gaudy mansion bristling with columns, capitals, and balconies, hidden behind high walls near Phnom Penh, Poan was in the act of paying the brothel owner, while little Seca, terrorized, was being held by one of the *Oknha*'s bodyguards. We were relieved to observe that the girl had not yet been raped. Arriving too late had been our worst fear on the way over from our headquarters.

Four days earlier, a local police officer, Lim Bunna, had alerted our unit of Seca's presence in the brothel. He said a girl working in the brothel, named Makara, had ventured to the police station to make a deposition concerning Seca. Makara had taken pity on her.

"Seca's mother sent her to Phnom Penh to work in a restaurant, but they were tricked," Makara said. "Seca does everything she can to avoid going with the clients, which really angers Madame Boppha, our *mama-san*. But she won't be able to resist for long because the owner paid for her. I'm afraid he's going to sell her to a client if the police don't help her."

Officer Bunna admitted he had almost neglected to alert us to her danger. "To tell the truth, I wasn't that troubled, even though the girl had tears in her eyes. I remember asking her if that's all she had to say. She got a bit miffed and told me, 'You know, most girls like us were lured in like that.' I replied something like, 'Brothels have always existed.' Then she said something that moved me. She asked me if I had a daughter, and I showed her a picture of my little *Srey*[21] Leap and told her she was 14. Makara sighed and said that was how old Seca was, too. 'We're all someone's daughter or sister or niece.' And she asked me if I would do something to help.

"After she left, I set her deposition on a pile of other papers. But that girl's visit had made me uncomfortable, and that night, I had a nightmare. I was walking along in the red-light district, where girls were hustling for clients in front of the karaoke bars. All of a sudden, I recognized one of them. It was my daughter, wearing heavy makeup. I was horrified. I shouted, 'What are you doing here?' When she saw me, she burst into tears. She said her boyfriend had sold her. Before I could reach her to pull her into my arms, a muscular man grabbed her, and they disappeared into the bar. When I woke up, I immediately thought of this girl Seca, and I decided to alert you."

As soon as he notified our unit, we went into battle mode. It was crucial to act rapidly and recover this adolescent before the irreparable was done, and put this inhumane businessman out of action. To ready an operation against his establishment, we needed a great deal of information about its configuration and personnel, so Bith Kim Hong, the new chief of the AHJTP, decided to send two men, one of whom was Lim Bunna, to infiltrate the brothel. We had temporarily reassigned Bunna to our team because he knew Makara. We figured that would help advance our investigation more quickly. Plus, he could let her know about the upcoming raid and she could help calm the other girls when we rushed in. For they would surely be frightened. To them, the police had usually represented blows and insults, not saviors.

Bunna and his colleague Keo Sovanna returned the next morning from their successful infiltration mission with a wealth of information about potential clients, and our unit was able to organize the operation down to the last detail.

Just before the raid, the chief assembled his team in the briefing room, where he told them to remember this was a rescue mission, not a normal raid. To bolster that intent, two social workers, Vong Naly and Chim Huy, would come with us to protect the girls during and right after the police action. He explained to these two women they would be responsible for watching over the girls, reassuring them and making sure they understood what was going on.

Then he addressed the team again, nodding at each member or group of members as he assigned their precise tasks:

"You two will photograph the premises and gather material evidence.

"You men will register the girls' belongings and put them in separate envelopes. Make sure you collect all their mobile phones right away. We don't want them to contact other people who could accidentally get implicated in the affair and complicate everything. But tell them they'll recover what belongs to them unless it's evidence for the accusations.

"You four, concentrate on making the arrests. We're looking for three security guards, the *mama-san* and the owner."

Huy interrupted the chief. "Sir, what happens to the girls afterwards?"

"I'm glad you asked that," Chief Hong said as he turned to two women hovering near the door. He motioned to them to enter the room, and then presented them:

"Sam Borey and Khim Maly. Borey is from the Department of Social Affairs."

"Hello," said Borey. "I'm a social assistant, and my team works with trafficking victims. The major asked us to take care of the girls you bring here tonight."

The chief gestured at Maly. "Would you like to introduce yourself?"

"Yes, of course. I fell victim myself to a procuring network when I was fifteen. A few years ago, I was rescued by the police during a raid. Now I'm studying and I work for a non-profit that helps reinsert girls. It's important that you understand how this situation affects them. They are victims, not criminals."

Chief Hong interrupted. "The operation Ms. Maly refers to was not exactly crowned with success. The charges ended up being dropped. But that was before we put our new procedures into place, and we made mistakes. Perhaps you can explain what happened, Ms. Maly?"

"It was a normal evening in the brothel," she said. "But then police suddenly appeared from every direction, waving guns and shouting questions. We had no idea what was going on, so we were terrified. They rounded up about fifty of us and brought us to the police station, then locked us in a tiny, horrible room not fit for an animal, and some of the officers took photos of us with their mobile phones. My picture ended up here."

She held up an old newspaper article with a picture of herself behind bars. "There was nothing to sleep on, no food or water. The brothel owner and the *mama-san* were in the cell next to us, and they spent the entire night cursing us and threatening us."

The chief stepped in again, speaking to the whole team. "That won't happen again! So, we have to work very closely with these women. In fact, I think it would be a good idea if all the girls benefited from a social worker to support them during the hearing process. My team will evaluate their needs. And we've set up safe places for each of them once they've been brought here."

Ready to launch the operation to liberate Seca, we took off. Once we got into our positions surrounding the brothel, we awaited the chief's signal to enter. We didn't know that Seca was about to leave it. The *mama-san* had dressed her in sexy clothes and applied heavy makeup before bringing her into the owner's office for a talk with him.

"I have a special mission for you," the owner said in a syrupy voice. "With one of our best clients. You won't disappoint me, will you?"

"Please don't make me do this," Seca begged him, but he turned away and ordered the *mama-san* to make sure she was ready to leave shortly. Madam Boppha pushed Seca out of the room and down the hall, followed by the owner. One of our agents was inside the brothel, disguised as a client. He was watching for this, and when he gave the order to raid, most of the squad converged on the entrance and rushed in, while officers armed with AK47 assault rifles guarded the other exits. Chaos erupted, and many of the girls, overwhelmed with the shock, started crying.

Huy, the social worker, reassured them, "Don't be afraid. We're here to help you."

The policemen opened all the doors and searched the rooms, then started taking pictures and collecting evidence. Our unit leader Mok Phaly and the officers assigned to making the arrests located Madam Boppha, but they couldn't find her boss. He was not inside, and none of the men posted at the exits had seen him leave. Worse, Seca was also missing.

The unit leader suddenly realized there might be an upper-story balcony with a fire exit, and Makara, who was also searching for Seca, confirmed there was one. They must have climbed down and escaped.

"Call all units!" the chief cried into his radio.

Several officers separated the *mama-san* and her guards from the girls, then loaded all twelve into buses and headed to the police station. Bunna was sadly disappointed when he realized Seca was not in the group.

He hurried over to the unit leader. "Is it too late? Did they sell Seca?"

"We'll keep looking," was all he got in reply.

The girls having reached the station, the two social workers took them under their wings, trying to answer all their questions at once. Were they free or not? Would they be charged? How were they going to support themselves and where could they live? They were worried, being so unused to making their own decisions about their lives.

"Here's what's going to happen," Huy explained. "We'll keep you here for a short time, no more than forty-eight hours, while we take your statements. The goal is to gather enough evidence to help the courts put your former bosses behind bars. We also want to find the best way to help you. We'll start by trying to contact your families."

Makara spoke up. "And if we don't want to go home?"

"In that case, we'll place you in safe lodgings. We're going to take care of you."

Meanwhile, the unit leader was questioning Madam Boppha in a small interrogation room.

"Where did the brothel owner bring Seca? Who is this client?"

But the *mama-san* fixed her gaze on the wall, lips firmly closed.

"If you help us now, it will go better for you in court," he said.

"I was just doing my job."

"I'll repeat it one last time – if you make the right choice now, maybe the judge will be more indulgent. If you refuse to save that child, it will cost you dearly!"

Madam Boppha reflected a long while, then suddenly grabbed the pencil and paper in front of her and scribbled some words on it.

"It's him. You'll find her there."

The unit chief returned to Bunna with a satisfied look on his face. "We have a name."

Bunna's heart bounded when he saw the name. "He's *Oknha*! One of the most influential businessmen in the city!"

"No matter," the unit chief said. "We have support from people at the highest levels. So don't be afraid of anything."

They immediately left with about a dozen men and drove to the address the *mama-san* had indicated. As the unit chief was about to knock on the front door, it opened, and he found himself face-to-face with the brothel owner.

"The law forbids the selling or procuring of a human being for sexual purposes, especially when it concerns a minor," the chief said, polite but firm.

The businessman Poan Sarin was watching the whole scene and as he stepped forward, they could see a young adolescent girl behind him.

"This is my niece! Isn't that so, Chenda?"

"My name is Seca," she mumbled, looking down. Then she suddenly pushed past him and lurched through the door, taking refuge behind the group of officers.

The *Oknha* pasted a saccharine smile on his face and tried to slip money into Phaly's hand.

"Sir, it seems there's been a misunderstanding," he said.

"Keep your cash for your lawyer, sir. You are both arrested."

As officers handcuffed the two criminals, Bunna grabbed Seca's hand.

"No need to worry now, it's all over," he said. "I promise to tell your mama how brave you were and how lucky she is to have a daughter like you."

People might say this story could only be fictional, that it's too good to be true, especially people who knew Cambodia in that epoch.

They're right.

Although inspired by true events, it was written for a film we would use to train the country's police officers. But this film represents something extraordinary, which I still marvel at today: the Ministry of the Interior validated it, even though Cambodians so often shift the blame for all evils befalling their country onto the shoulders of foreigners, widely thought to behave like sexual predators. It also demonstrates, uncompromisingly, that the high and mighty can be corrupters, that they will try to profit from impunity, and that the police are susceptible to being bought.

In the beginning stages of the Project, a video like that would never have been accepted by the police hierarchy, let alone used for training. They would have criticized it for "putting into question Khmer honor and dignity." It was produced only after our unit had existed for several years and real progress had been made in fighting pedocriminals.

Its validation showed that up to the highest levels, it was understood that nothing could be more honorable and dignified than protecting children from this kind of trafficking and crime, and that all were obliged to recognize the humiliating defects of Cambodian society.

We knew we would not be able to save every "Little Flower" like Seca, or incarcerate every powerful man who abused them, but this fictional story expressed our commitment to it, and bid the entire police institution to share that commitment.

I couldn't have asked for anything better.

VII - Letters to Nary, Sokha, Chen, Pech, Oeun, May, Bopha and Sophea

Nary, Sokha, Chhen, Pech, Oeun, May, Bopha, Sophea – what has become of you? Our lives crossed in such dramatic circumstances I have never forgotten you. You were such young girls, and you had been raped, your lives broken like trampled, once-beautiful flowers. Two of you were almost killed by your aggressors.

Today, you must be in your twenties or thirties. Have any of you overcome the horrible shock of your attack? Have you been able to love, and be loved? Have you been able to start a family?

These questions still haunt me, and always will.

Dear Nary,

Nary, I first saw you when our Landcruiser, covered in red laterite dust, entered the courtyard of the Sisophon[22] commissariat. I had arrived with my colleagues Sar Darun and Kong Sun to give a hands-on training session based on case studies. I also wanted to address some of the difficulties the local police were encountering in this isolated province bordering Thailand.

When I got out of the car, I realized our case study would not be a fictitious one this time, and that, sadly, we were about to confront the revolting criminal brutality of a man against an 8-year-old child.

A woman, your mother, was sitting on the tile floor under an awning, her head on her knees, eyes down. You and your brother, both looking frail and undernourished, sat side by side on the other side of the courtyard, arms tightly enlaced. Your feet were bare, Nary, and you wore a ragged blouse and a red and white skirt spattered with mud. A makeshift bandage covered a large wound on your neck.

You and your mother had just been interviewed by investigators from our local unit, directed by a remarkable woman, Captain Meas Dany. The chief of a police station thirty miles from the provincial capital had alerted her unit of the attack, and as soon as she had completed the procedural actions and organized the arrest of your rapist, she had called to inform me. I went straight to work on the case as soon as we arrived.

Your mother told us she had been living with you and your brother in a makeshift tent covered with a tarp, ever since your father abandoned her to go live with a younger woman. One recent evening – she couldn't remember the exact day – you wandered away to gather wood. A man hiding in the bamboo forest had sprung at you, and gripping your delicate throat, pulled you to the edge of the river parallel to the marketplace. There, on the dusty ground only a few dozen yards from your mother and brother, he savagely raped. Then, he threw you into the river and walked away, figuring you were so wounded you would drown. But you managed to grab a branch, you hung on and pulled yourself out of the river, and you survived.

You received no medical care. Your mother had simply cleaned the wound on your neck and wiped the blood from your legs. There was no doctor in the village, and you had no money to pay the fees anyway.

The policewoman had interviewed you with great tenderness, but you related the facts of this terrible aggression with difficulty, in a low voice. You answered her questions only with nods of your head: yes, you were afraid he was going to strangle you; yes, he tried to drown you in the river; yes, you felt bad pain between your thighs.

A policeman interviewed your brother with the same patience. Then they brought you rice, fruit, and water, and spoke to you gently about insignificant things to distract you from the violent images obviously swirling through your head.

At that moment, I felt our hard work had not been in vain – all the training sessions, the case follow-up missions, the equipment we'd secured, the efforts to sensitize the authorities, enlist social services and so much more. I was content because I felt it had been a success. You had survived, your story was confirmed, the prosecutor informed and the perpetrator of this horrible act, who had now been identified, would be arrested as soon as the police got a warrant to bring him in.

He not only inflicted pain and trauma on you, Nary, but he made you an orphan, even though you had a mother.

"I can't bring her back to the village after what's happened," she told the police. "I'm too ashamed."

Hearing that gave me a terrible shock. Perhaps that's why I remember you and your drama so vividly out of the many hundreds of cases we handled. How could your own mother worry more about what the villagers might think than of your future? And these people whose glances she dreaded – how could they possibly spurn you, a little girl who had been raped, and reject you as if you were responsible for the vile aggression you had endured?

I don't want to hear about "culture, civilization, traditions" to explain the horrendous injustice of that. To not feel compassion for a raped child is to negate every form of civilization. Your mother's attitude infuriated me. But there had to be some kind of explanation for it. Was misery exacerbating her soul's imperfections? Or did she hope that by abandoning you, and your brother too, she was trying to give you the chance for a happier life? Because if you stayed with her, you were condemned to a somber future. That conjecture seemed difficult to swallow.

The unit chief asked for my advice. "The boy doesn't want to leave his sister. Do you have any idea what we can do with them? The little girl should be examined right away. We're going to bring her to my doctor, but what then?"

There was no orphanage in the area, only two centers that took in young teenagers.

Suddenly, a spark lit up my black thoughts – there might be a solution. I recalled I had organized the extrication of a young Cambodian girl called upon by the Criminal Court of Paris to testify against the former director of an NGO who had abused her. His friends had attempted everything they could to prevent her from leaving the country, but after an ordeal I can only compare to a good spy movie, we got her on a plane and before a judge in Paris. Her aggressor, a French citizen, was condemned for the crime. This same NGO group had survived the scandal, and I knew they had several centers to receive orphans, including one in this region. I called their main office to explain the situation.

"Don't worry about a thing," the executive director said. "We have an orphanage in Battambang. Bring the two children there, and I'll alert its administrator."

How happy I was to announce this good news to the police officers! They were then able to reassure you, saying, "Nary, it's over. You and your brother are saved. You can stay together, you will go to school, you will no longer be hungry, and you'll live in security."

From one minute to the next, your life and that of your brother branched toward a new horizon. You would find acceptable living conditions in that orphanage, organized in the form of family homes that each sheltered ten or so children and a "mama" who was responsible for them. This confirms, Nary, what my colleague Kong Sun so often repeated, that our future might be written, but we don't know what the words are.

Your attacker was arrested the day following your interview. Your village chief knew how closely the prosecutor was following your case, and he grew alarmed by the gravity of what he had first considered "a mere incident." He identified the suspect, who had committed the same kind of sexual aggression before. If the villagers had considered his actions more seriously, if they had stopped him then instead of ignoring him, you would not have gone through that hell.

Will you ever read these lines, Nary? I doubt it. I wish I hadn't lost track of you. I could have stayed in touch, since I know the leaders of the NGO that took you and your brother in. But, once I was back in Phnom Penh, other cases awaited me, always another and another. In this kind of work, we haven't much time to indulge in sentiment. I feel compassion for every victim like you, but the most important thing for us is to keep up with our investigations. We do our best every time, but we don't always win, and then yet another case comes up. We treat all of them with the same determination, but also with a certain pragmatism. We can't change the world, but we can fight against its revolting social disorders, and act instead of sitting back and brooding about it.

Dear Sokha,

You almost didn't survive being raped either, Sokha. It was eight in the morning the day it happened, when a neighbor, a man in his mid-forties, invited you to gather green mangoes in his garden. His name was Pram To, and he had been a soldier, and now worked as a carpenter in your tiny village in Battambang.

You were 12 years old, and you thought only to please your mother by bringing her some of these delicious fruits. So, without any misgiving, you followed him and then climbed into a tree in his garden to choose the best mangoes.

But when you got back down, carrying the mangoes in the hollow of your skirt, Pram grabbed your arm and dragged you toward an outbuilding on his farm. You screamed, and the mangoes fell on the ground as you fought against him with all your force. The man was strong though, and he grabbed you by the neck and hit your face, then squeezed your throat, fragile as that of a bird. Your struggling infuriated him.

"I'll kill you if you shout again!"

Fearing for your life, you pretended to lose consciousness. Pram tore your clothing off and raped you for over an hour. Your eyes were closed, your teeth clenched. Realizing you were awake, and hearing your groans, he smashed your head against the ground, then hit you again, this time with a piece of wood.

Believing you were dead, he dragged you into a bushy area behind the farm and left you there before running away from the village. You were covered with blood, but alive. As soon as you felt you were out of danger, you got up and despite the pain, you limped back to your mother, who was with your sister at a nearby sewing work shop, and you told her what had happened.

Three hours later, your neighbor was arrested for rape and attempted murder. At first, he denied it all, his face red with anger. But everything pointed to his guilt: your medical exam, the evidence report from the crime scene, the blood on his clothes and body. In the end he confessed, but only after trying to bribe his way out with promises of money. Your mother held to the complaint she had filed, and he was sentenced to ten years in prison and ordered to pay damages to you and your family.

Although this happened fifteen years ago, I would like to render homage to your wisdom, Sokha. You faced a callous, violent brute with a courage that demands respect. I'd also like to honor your family's exemplary behavior in reporting the crime and making no concessions to your rapist. To any readers who are surprised to see this kind of behavior qualified as exemplary, I must remind them that back then, poor families often thought long and hard before bringing an affair like that to the police and the courts, favoring a "friendly arrangement" instead. For even if they could reasonably expect a child rapist to be condemned by the penal system, they had no guarantee that any court-allocated compensation would actually be paid. Also, choosing to compromise guaranteed them peace, while holding fast to a complaint exposed them to the guilty party's vengeance or that of his family's. We often saw victims compelled to move to a different province to protect themselves and their families.

Although understandable, this tendency to avoid filing a complaint or dropping it in exchange for compensation made our unit's mission much more difficult. Our main goal was to put pedophiles behind bars, and thereby protect society, and that meant getting the cooperation of victims and their families. So wherever you are today, Sokha, be sure that you and your family's refusal to negotiate with the man who raped you has contributed to protecting other children.

Impunity encourages people to commit – and repeat – criminal acts. By scorning financial interests, by shrugging off the lead weight of custom, you helped reduce that impunity.

For that, you have my respect.

Dear Chen,

Not all rapists use brute force to abuse children. Some take advantage of the confidence those children have placed in them. As in your case, Chen, when your father's cousin, the man you called "Uncle," started sexually abusing you when you were only five years old.

The first time, you were playing outside the house when he gently led you to a small building in the farmyard. There, he touched you, caressed you, then raped you.

"When you're big, it won't hurt at all, so don't worry," he told you with a smile. "And don't ever say anything to anybody. It's our little secret. If you talk, your dad will kill me and then he'll kick you out of the house."

You were in shock and very scared. Your world had turned upside down; it was now a place of pain and fear. A few weeks later, he did it again in a hammock slung between two trees. Then a third time, on a day of heavy rains in September. It always hurt, and that last time, the pain was so great it overcame your fear. You told your mother what happened.

That very afternoon, the police turned up at "Uncle's" home only a few hundred yards from yours. Before they had even begun gathering evidence or called in experts, the man blithely confessed everything, as if he had no consciousness of the magnitude of what he had done to you. As if it had all been a game. You were confided to an NGO specialized in supporting women and children who are victims of violence. You're twenty now and I would so like to know you are safe in the arms of someone who loves you and helps you forget the wounds of your childhood.

Dear Pech and Ouen,

Pech and Ouen, your attacker got to you by drugging you. You were both thirteen in October 2005 when you left your village in Kampot province to go live in a small village between Sisophon and Poipet near the Thai border. A woman close to your families had found jobs for you with a farmer there whose property was on the border. You were supposed to earn 1,500 Thai bahts[23] a month – not a lot, but you would be fed and lodged, and the salary would help your relatives.

The farmer, Sinh Boram, was a tall robust man, darkly tanned like most country dwellers. One day, he took you with him to cut grass in a spot far from the farm and village. The plan was to spend the night there in a hut by the fields.

It was the beginning of November, and after the long day of fieldwork, night had fallen around six o'clock. No rain, and it was nice and warm in the hut. It had no electricity, no mosquito nets, no beds, but there was a mat on the floor, where you both fell into a heavy sleep, so heavy that your boss was able to undress you, fondle you and rape you, one after the other, without even waking you. Incapable of putting up the slightest resistance, there were no screams, no struggles. You were like floppy dolls in the hands of a sex maniac. Why? He had drugged you by slipping some GHB into your food. A friend of his in Bangkok had supplied it, the rapist's drug of choice because it is odorless and colorless in its liquid form and can easily be poured into a soup or a drink. Usually, its anesthetizing effect makes the victim extremely lethargic, as if drunk, and as it wears off only gradually, it leaves little or no memory of what happened while under its influence. But Sinh had increased the dose so much it sent you both into a coma-like sleep.

You came out of your torpor first, Pech, and you woke up your friend. It took several minutes to regain your senses, but you soon realized what had happened to you. Knowing you were far from everything, as good as prisoners in your vile employer's hands, you decided to say nothing and pretend like all was normal.

"Come along, girls, time to go home," he had shouted just after dawn. And you took the road back, chatting as usual, while the farmer went along his way, a delighted smile on his face, like that of someone who'd taken a gamble and won.

Even though you were so young, you showed great force of character. You were determined your rapist would pay for his crime. When you got back to the farm, you found an excuse to go into the village, Pech, and you called your uncle, who worked in a restaurant in Poipet, only about six miles away. You told him how your boss had sexually abused you and Ouen. Your uncle contacted your parents, and they went to the farm right away. Without addressing the farmer, they brought you to the police commissary to file a complaint. The police went to Sinh's farm. He did not deny the sexual relations but defended himself vehemently.

"They agreed to it because I promised them 500 bahts each. Here's the money, by the way!"

He tried to push the bills into your hands, but you refused, exclaiming, "That's a lie – he drugged us, then raped us!"

The farmer was one of those people who think everything and everyone has a price, especially when it involves the poor, and he insisted, "Be reasonable and take the money!"

The argument got heated, and Sinh was arrested and brought to jail. A search warrant was issued to search his house, and they found two small vials of a suspicious substance.

After being interrogated for several hours, the man capitulated and admitted he had raped you after administering the drug. Medical exams done in the hospital and analysis of the substance rounded out the body of evidence, leading to Sinh being sentenced to ten years in prison and liable for compensatory damages to the equivalent of 3,000 dollars for each of you.

Rumor has it this rapist was released after serving only eighteen months. If that is true, the people who managed to get him freed, most likely for a bribe of a handful of dollars, have made themselves accomplices to an unforgivable form of tolerance toward sexual crimes against children.

Please know, Pech and Ouen, that this is totally unacceptable in my eyes.

Dear May,

As for you, May, you were only five years old when a couple of teenage boys stole your precious childhood innocence from you.

You were at a wedding with your mother and brother when Sna Chann, a 16-year-old, took you by the hand as if to have a dance. But instead of going to the dance floor, he led you to a dark isolated spot and started to touch you under your dress before penetrating you, first with his finger then with his penis. The other boy, a 14-year-old named Pean Koun came out just then and he also raped you.

"Why are you hurting me?" you cried, panic-stricken. "Where is my mama and my brother?"

You got away from them and limped awkwardly back toward the brightly lit area, where some people saw you, a broken little flower, and they noticed one of your attackers slink away. Their description of the suspects helped lead to their being arrested the next day. Medical exams clearly showed the acts of penetration with violence you had endured, May, but at the juvenile court hearing, the case was requalified as "indecent acts" toward a child. The judge sentenced Sna to educational monitoring and released him, and his friend Pean, because of his age, was discharged after being admonished.

Your country at that time was in the course of widespread reconstruction, and courts for juveniles and the whole panoply of measures for specialized education were barely in the early development stages. Did those two boys ever truly understand the gravity of what they had inflicted on you? Probably not. I can only hope they did not repeat their offenses, but that's doubtful. Unless the perpetrators of an act so grave are punished, and then closely monitored with probation and education, I think the risk is great they will commit it again. Punishment dissuades violence of all kinds, including attacks on children due to sexual perversion. And without special educational measures, recidivism is extremely frequent. If given a choice, I would have judged on the side of severity: punishment, reeducation, psychological follow-up and then, possibly, probation. Only after a criminal demonstrates a genuine change in behavior should he merit a place in society. But judiciary systems that insist too much on reinsertion only condemn this type of criminal after giving numerous warnings. This is a mistake, and it's happening around the world. Judges need to give more consideration to victims, to recovery and to requiring due compensation for the damage done. When sex offenders like Sna and Pean are carelessly released, other innocent people, perhaps children as young as you were, are exposed to their predation.

I know that horrible experience radically changed your life, May. Then, during the social inquiry, your mother admitted she could no longer support her children because her husband had abandoned her in poverty, so you and your brother were placed in a home for children in Kampong Cham.

You must be about 20 years old now, May, and I fervently want to believe in your rebirth into a life without pain and loss.

Dear Bopha and Sophea,

My last letter is to you, Bopha and Sophea, because you had to overcome the worst of sexual crimes against children: incest. The worst because it is committed by the person who should have loved you with the deepest parental love, who should have guided you toward an awakening to life and prepared you with benevolent authority to become an adult. The worst because, to put an end to the horror, you had to denounce your own father as a pedophile, first to your mother, then to the police, then to the entire world. The worst because you had to resist your shameful father's blackmailing, phrases like: "if you say anything, you'll lose your family, you'll have nothing, you'll be alone in life, without your mother, without anything."

The man who gave you life threatened you with death.

The media related cases of incest from time to time, but our department's services were rarely solicited to deal with them. They were mostly handled by local police who, when they were informed, acted...as they pleased.

You were 19, Bopha, and you 16, Sophea, when you finally broke the silence.

Your family lived in a small house outside the town of Battambang. Your father took care of buffalo and other animals on his small farm while your mother went to the market nearly every day to sell water chestnuts. Taking advantage of his wife's daily absence, your father started abusing you when you were about 10, Bopha, and a few years later, he started in on your sister too.

But one June day in 2003, your mother suddenly started having bad stomach pain, so she confided her market stall to one of her sisters and returned home. To her stupefaction, she surprised her husband in bed with you, Sophea, crushing you with the length of his body.

You were 15. In a panic, you simply stared at your mother, terrified at what she was looking at, then you jumped up and rushed to a corner of the room, where you curled up in a ball, your feet under your skirt. Your father had sent your big sister to gather wood for the midday meal and the trap had closed on you that time.

In front of your mother, your father stood up, readjusted his clothes and put his palms together in a sign of submission before offering profuse apologies.

"Please forgive me! I couldn't resist my impulses. It's as if an evil spirit pushed me to it. It will never happen again."

Overwhelmed, your mother did not know what to do. She spoke to you and your sister for a long time and found out this had been going on for many years.

"He told us it was normal, that it happens in all families, but we could never tell anyone about it," you explained to her. "Otherwise, he would kill us both, because these things have to remain secret."

Your mother knew your father's behavior was criminal, but talking about it in public would engulf the family and all their relatives in shame, and maybe he would even go to jail. In any case, she would be left all alone, as would you. She decided she would try to forgive him, but hardly a week later, he raped you, Bopha, and you immediately reported it to her. You just couldn't keep living that way after so long, never daring to speak, never daring to resist.

Your mother did not hesitate a second longer. She confided in a lawyer who worked for the protection of children in Battambang. It took courage for your mother to denounce your father. She realized her life would crumble to pieces, irrevocably, and at that instant her heart must have started racing. A multitude of questions must have started spinning through her head.

"How will the police and the judges receive me? Will they believe me or mock me? What will the family say, and the neighbors? Who will take care of the farm, of my family, of my sick mother, and what about my business?"

She realized too that she would have to face a life of solitude, and that you, her daughters, would risk being rejected and loathed by boys their age. There were no answers, no comforting platitudes, but she did not back down. Joined by the lawyer, she went to the police and filed a complaint.

And you, Bopha and Sophea, finally liberated from that terrible repression, you responded to all their questions, hiding nothing during your interviews.

When the police pulled up in front of your house, your father tried to win their sympathy by welcoming them with a smile.

"What's going on?" he asked, all innocence.

"We'll discuss it at the station," an officer said. There was no smile on his face.

During questioning, your father tried to minimize his actions for a good while, but finally he confessed, pulling out his old excuse of "uncontrollable impulses provoked by evil spirits." But later, before the judge in the Battambang court, he could only stammer, "I don't know what to say...I can't say anything."

During the trial, you both called him an "animal" and demanded he be sent to prison for life. But the judge saw fit to sentence him to only eighteen and a half years as punishment for his unspeakable and unforgivable crime.

Once he was behind bars, you were both taken in by an NGO to learn the trade of seamstress. Your mother continued in her business.

I wonder if you have found husbands, and started families? I fervently hope the answer is "yes," for I know how painful loneliness can be.

In Cambodia, as elsewhere, many children, mostly girls, have endured the assaults of an incestuous father, whether biological or a stepfather. But very few of these cases are reported to the police. Because incest, there as elsewhere, in rich or poor families, is a crime that often gets buried, shut within the walls of the family home, imposing the victim's silence and very often that of the whole family.

Without the word of the victim, a family member, or the family's entourage to break that wall of silence, the police cannot act. And when a case of incest is confided to us, we must double our vigilance throughout our investigation, for the world of a family weighed down by this crime is one of pitfalls and snares in which truths and lies can tangle to the point of being inextricable.

Bopha and Sophea, your father's conviction stands out as an example for Cambodia, and for the entire world. The first person to thank for this is not the judge, but your mother. She helped you to a new life, and to you and other victims of this kind of crime, without even knowing it, she gave the gift of hope.

VIII - On the Trail of Human Traffickers

I will never forget the sight of those children squatting barefoot on the muddy ground around the huge piles of fish they were working on. Cambodian children, without a doubt. But they were just across the border in Thailand when I noticed them as I was crossing the frontier at Poipet. This was well before the struggle against child trafficking had become part of my primary mission; at this time, I was still leading international police cooperation at the French embassy.

In the border area of Poipet, a monumental disorder reigned against a filthy, wretched background. Huge bundles of merchandise were being carried into Thailand on men's backs or in rudimentary carts. A stream of taxis, pick-ups, and minivans, one more dilapidated than the next, were also convoying big bundles to the border, and once unloaded, they headed back to bring in more loads. Urgent deliveries crisscrossed through all this traffic. A tropical Grand Bazaar at rush hour, exposed to the blistering sun from morning 'til night, where dust, exhaust fumes, and the miasma of rotten fish and rummaged trash swirled and hung in the air, where horns honked in fury and shouting constantly resounded. Hundreds of porters milled about when they weren't curled up asleep on their jealously claimed parcel of pavement or dirt, or disputing over who would get to carry a bundle of goods.

A quarter of an hour of this and a person was reduced to bewilderment.

Oblivious to this havoc, the children sat in silence, grabbing the little fish mechanically. With a scaling knife, they chopped off the head and tail and gutted each fish, rinsed, then tossed them onto a pile. Over and over again. The fish were slated to be transformed into *prahok*, a sour and spicy fermented paste that serves as the national condiment of Cambodia.

These boys and girls, who looked to be from 8 to 12 years old, began at dawn and repeated the same gestures all day long to gain 50 bahts a day. Riveted to their never-ending piles of fish, what are these children if not slaves? Where did they come from, and who brought them to Thailand?

Some of them probably lived with their families on the Cambodian side and crossed the border morning and evening after handing over a small "fee" to the security guards. But others among the fifty or so children had doubtless come from far-off provinces.

How had their parents been talked into letting them leave home? Had they "sold" them? Or were they orphans or street kids who had been duped, or even kidnapped? I never found out, but it was clear they came from poor families.

If I had questioned the man employing them and the intermediaries who had arranged their passage to Thailand, they would have all sung the same song, the one used by most men and women who go into human trafficking: "By giving them a job, I help their families, and raise them out of poverty. These kids have to work in order to eat, and that's just how it is in Cambodia for the poorest of us. You wouldn't understand."

And I would counter, "You're no benefactor of humanity! You're a trafficker or an accomplice of traffickers of human beings, and you're exploiting these children for your own profit."

Upon hearing this nasty word "trafficker," they would have stood aghast and protested, "Trafficker? Not at all! I may have helped them sneak into Thailand, but that's it."

It's true that illegally entering a foreign country by hiring a smuggler or using false papers doesn't necessarily make you a trafficking victim. Most emigrants leave their countries to find a better life or flee famine or war, and they go voluntarily. The smugglers they pay can and should be pursued for aiding illegal immigration and for putting the life of another person into danger, but they can't automatically be accused of human trafficking.

Trafficking implies a lie, trickery, where the displaced person ends up exploited, sexually or in forced labor in his native country or abroad. And at least some of these young fish scalers must have been trafficking victims, who never imagined they would be expected to spend their childhood squatting next to a big pile of fish, compelled to chop, gut, rinse and repeat ad nauseam.

Aside from forced labor, particularly common among the men on fishing boats in Thailand, exploitation in the sex industry was the principal source of local and international trafficking cases our unit had to deal with. Each one presented a different aspect, but they all began with a false promise of a better life somewhere else, either in Phnom Penh or in a foreign country. The primary targets for traffickers were young mothers abandoned by their husbands and girls whose parents were mired in poverty and debt.

The promised scenario was always based on a lie, and exploitation, most often sexual exploitation, was always the result. The driving forces? For the victims, desperation, ignorance, and fear; for the traffickers, pure and simple greed.

As soon as our hotline was up and running, we started getting calls, and the number of human trafficking cases grew larger every week. Some led to nothing, but others led to arrests. Like the call we received from a Vietnamese man who repaired and rented batteries. He thought a Vietnamese couple had begun trafficking young girls for prostitution in Phnom Penh.

His tip delivered a 17-year-old Vietnamese girl named Vin Thi from a life she had never chosen.

Her mother, Vin Ang, brought her to Phnom Penh in November 2001 from their impoverished, remote village in the Mekong delta. Ang had heard that many Western residents working in international cooperation in the capital were looking for Vietnamese housekeepers, reputed to be more competent and better educated than Cambodian country girls. Through some people in her village, she got in touch with a woman from Phnom Penh, a certain Kham Thuy, who promised her she would find work for Thi. Ang brought her daughter to speak to the woman in person, who assured her it was all above board.

"It's my job to place young girls in good families, after giving them a short training about their future work," said Kham. "You can rest easy, as your girl seems bright, and should soon be able to start working and sending you money to help you."

"It seems all right, but I must set one condition," Ang insisted. "I want my daughter to work only as a house cleaner, or if possible, a cook, and not as a server in a bar. Just because we're poor doesn't mean my girl should do just anything."

"Don't worry, I'll take care of her. Plus, she can sleep here – we have a little bedroom for girls in training. Another one is going to arrive tomorrow in fact. You can go home to Vietnam without a care. You'll see results by the *Tết*[24] holidays."

Ang hesitated. "In that case, could you please give me an advance on her salary, for my return trip and food for my other kids?"

And she accepted the 250 dollars Kham gave her. Big mistake. Now, Ang was bound by a debt and her daughter was the security. The sum represented several months of pay, which would be nearly impossible to reimburse in case of any problem. But Kham inspired confidence. Her gray hair and respectable manner, her well-kept shophouse were all calculated to do just that, masking her true role as one thread in a complex web of deceit.

Hardly had her mother left when the woman's face hardened.

"You, go rest in the bedroom," she told Thi. "I'll be back soon."

Thi suddenly felt uneasy. Why had Kham's face changed that way? She did not dare say a word though. Realizing she was all alone in an unknown place, far from her home, friends, or family, and that her sole contact was this woman Kham, her unease turned to anxiety. She was hungry and she wondered when they would eat. She drank some water from the sink in the room and sat down on the small bed, where she waited for what seemed a long time. Suddenly the light, a bare bulb hanging from the ceiling, went out, and since there was no window in the little room, she stumbled over to the door. To her surprise, she found it locked.

Fear and anguish filled her, but finally, overcome with fatigue, she lay on the bed. Soon after, she heard voices in the outer apartment. The door opened and Kham appeared, accompanied by an older man, Mok Heng, whose round belly jiggled against his tight red shirt, and a young woman named Yun Sau, who had long hair and wore heavy makeup.

"You're going to come with us," Yun said. "We'll take care of you."

She spoke in Vietnamese, which reassured Thi slightly, as she had been thinking, ever since her mother left, that something ominous was happening to her.

Kham's face wore a fixed smile. "You didn't think I gave your mama all that money for nothing, did you? Get up. They'll explain what's going to happen next."

"But what about my training to be a housecleaner?" Thi asked.

The man gripped her arm and said, "Come on, let's go!"

Hundred-dollar bills changed hands and Thi found herself in the back of a hulking black Landcruiser with tinted windows. The trip did not take long. They pulled up in the courtyard of a villa on a dark road near the riverbanks.

"Go in with the other girls, and tonight you start your new job," Mok said. "Do what people tell you to do, or I'll dump you in the Mekong, right there. And shut up about it!"

She wasn't a child, and she had begun to understand what was going on. So, the stories she'd heard in the countryside were true. She wondered if her mother had known.

The couple pushed her into a large room encumbered with mattresses and suitcases. In the back was a toilet area open to the room, with a sink, a mirror and a jumble of beauty products and accessories. A shower head dripped water on a tiled floor.

Four girls were sitting cross-legged on a mat, eating.

"Come sit down," one of them said. "And hurry. They'll be back soon to take us to the bar. Eat something, but fast, then you better take a shower. We'll give you some new clothes. You're light-skinned, so you'll be a success."

She lowered her head. Her heart was beating like a drum, even though she was exhausted. She knew she no longer had a choice.

When the couple returned, they were ready. The five girls crowded into the back of the Landcruiser, and seeing how scared Thi looked, one of them tried to reassure her by whispering, "Don't worry, just do what we do. You'll get used to it."

Then she found herself in a bar, engulfed in loud music. It was full of male customers who were to be persuaded to drink, and perhaps "entertained." Yun and Mok had come in with them, and the long-haired woman established herself behind a large counter, while her partner sat at a table and started chatting with customers.

Thi was trapped, like so many other girls her age. She thought about running away, but that seemed impossible. Where could she go? She had to resign herself to her situation.

But that was not to be her fate, thanks to the conscientious battery repairman who called our hotline. His information triggered a police operation, which we meticulously organized in Phnom Penh from the office of Police Commander Phuong Phalit, who oversaw the special unit there. My role was to lend support and guidance, and make sure the operation respected our procedural rules. I also had to verify arrangements with social services and certain NGOs, to take any eventual victims under their wings.

Directed by Commander Phuong, the intervention brought together eight officers, including three women. Armed with the prosecutor's authorization, they started out at nine in the evening. The city was quiet at that hour, the traffic calmer, but the bars and the brothels masquerading as massage parlors were at their most animated. When the police turned into the lane where this particular bar was located, they saw a crowd of people at its only entrance, so they parked at the far end. They had to act fast. They approached discreetly, then broke into a run, rushing both sides of the entrance. Two of them pinned the bouncers at the door, and the other officers pushed their way inside. When they shouted "Police!" no one moved for a second, but then everyone started shouting and running in every direction.

This moment was always the most delicate for the police, for they had to separate the girls and lead them to safety, but at the same time arrest the personnel in the establishment and detain any clients. These had to be identified, then shown the door – a summons to appear in court the following day in hand.

Once the ruckus had calmed down, the police gradually cleared out the premises, bringing the suspects to the station in one vehicle, and the young women and girls in another so they could give their statements and meet with the social workers.

Yun Sau and Mok Heng were arrested for complicity in human trafficking, kidnapping, and procuring, and were eventually sent to jail along with Kham Thuy, their intermediary. The woman who had served as a contact in the source region, where Thi and her family lived, was identified and arrested by the Vietnamese police.

All five girls were confided to a charitable organization, but three of them left its safehouse that same night to resume their work in a different bar. Thi and another girl, Sreng Mai, also a trafficking victim of this network, stayed put. They ended up becoming best friends, and were able to pursue English language studies with plans to work in a shop or even in a bank.

Thi told me she had a hard time forgiving her mother for leaving her alone in Phnom Penh with the woman Kham Thuy. Shouldn't her mother have anticipated what might happen to her? Was it possible she had sold her? The idea made her skin crawl. Still, Ang was her mother, and she was so poor that Thi vowed to send her some money once she had gotten on her feet.

This case shows an international human trafficking network isn't necessarily an elaborate ring of dozens of criminals. The leaders Yun and Mok, the intermediary Kham and the contact in Cambodia were all it took to keep a ruthless trafficking business spinning along.

Some of the trafficking cases we handled proved to be the work of even more rudimentary organizations. One such turned up in the border town of Poipet.

Casinos there were known for laundering money, and each vied for the top prize in wringing their betting clients dry. Although casinos are officially banned to Cambodians, they are open to all the other gamblers of Asia, and because of that, Poipet, a little Vegas, catered to any other vices their clients might wish to indulge in.

One enterprising Cambodian woman, Kanika Massa, a 25-year-old masseuse, profited by this to open a "relaxation salon" in 2005. She aimed to attract as many salon patrons from the incessant flow of gamblers as she could, and she succeeded so well that one day she found herself in need of "fresh meat." Being the type of person to avoid complicating her life, she simply went off in search of new girls herself. She headed to a village in Siem Reap province, where she figured she could find plenty of young, pretty girls, and most important for her purposes, from impoverished families.

Pretending she was about to open a laundromat, she soon recruited five girls from 15 to 19 years old. She easily convinced their parents by promising to pay them 80 dollars a month to employ their daughters in easy work: removing clothes from washing machines, then drying and ironing them. Plus, the girls would get free food and lodging. And since Kanika never skimped when it came to chumming the waters with enticing bait, she added a bonus of time off to celebrate *Pchum Ben*, when Cambodians honor their ancestors and present food offerings. This week-long festival cannot be missed, or the enraged spirits of their deceased relatives will torment them for an entire year. They believe phantoms exist as surely as the living do, and you don't play around with the spirits.

Kanika returned to Poipet with her prizes, mentally counting the wads of dollars her "stock" was sure to bring her. All the girls exulted at the idea of a future unlike the one they'd expected as a peasant's wife deep in the countryside, most likely a life of drudgery and poverty.

Once they arrived, their joy evaporated. There was no laundromat, only a building sporting a big sign: "Kanika Massa Massage Parlor." As they walked in, two men met them. One was a young man in military fatigues with an automatic rifle slung across his shoulder, the other an older man, Kanika's husband, who looked them over from head to toe, then grunted approval.

"If you shout or try to run off, you'll pay for it," he said. "If you're friendly with the clients, you'll be fine, and you'll get the salary you were promised. The girls who work here already will explain how it works, and they'll give you your outfits."

Eight girls, who were a bit older than the new batch, worked in the massage parlor, which had a large barroom and about a dozen cubicles equipped with mattresses, massage oils, and in plain sight on nightstands, boxes of condoms. The five new girls protested and tried to push their way toward the exit, but the two men roughly held them back. They were caught in the net. From now on, their life would be drinking with clients, massaging them, and having sex with them.

But two weeks later, one of the five new girls managed to run away. A client had paid to have her in his hotel room for three hours, so the salon's guard brought her there. The minute his back was turned, she grabbed her chance, hailing a tuk-tuk to take her to her village, over thirty miles away. Her family alerted the local police, who reported the crime to our unit in Beantey Meanchey province, and our task force opened a case based on her complaint.

Two days later, the police arrested Kanika, her husband and their henchmen, and rescued the four other trafficking victims. The massage parlor closed and the other women working there went their separate ways.

A "happy ending" you might say, just like in a Hollywood film. Not exactly. Reality doesn't always coincide with the cliches some screenwriters rely on. In a dramatic twist, only two of the five girls chose to go back to their native villages. The three others, who were over 18, chose to take jobs in other massage parlors, where they negotiated better conditions for themselves. Was their choice dictated by the fear of living in shame for the rest of their lives among their own relatives and neighbors, by the possibility of never finding husbands because of it? Yes, at least to some extent. But like many young women in Cambodia, they also figured they could earn more money in massage and sexual services than in a factory or as a housecleaner.

The reason these trafficking victims had escaped their jailers so quickly was because they had remained in Cambodia. Their rescue would have been far more complicated and doubtful if they had fallen into the clutches of Lam Thy, a Vietnamese woman from Malaysia, and Baang Maryan, a Cambodian woman from Takeo. These two would have put the young girls under lock and key, then brought them across the Gulf of Thailand to force them to work in brothels in George Town on the Malay Peninsula, like some of their other victims.

Our department investigated these two women in 2004, and after following their movements for over two months, we had enough proof to arrest them. Their business was ghastly: They exported babies, children, and adolescent girls to Malaysia.

The babies were sold to childless Malaysian couples. Baang "stocked up" in her native province, buying babies from poor families by assuring them they would be placed in rich homes in Phnom Penh where their mothers could visit them twice a year. This was a lie. In fact, they were smuggled to Malaysia via Thailand. Baang's cousin Sarin Thao served as conveyor. At the start of each two-day voyage, Baang drugged two or three of the babies with herbal infusions, then swaddled them in cotton wrappings and tucked them among bundles of merchandise on the back seat of Sarin's Landcruiser. The departure point of this long journey was about eight miles northwest of Phnom Penh. The two cousins headed to the Thai border toward Bangkok then south to Pattani where they crossed into Malaysia, always timing it to arrive at night. Over 1200 miles, taking 30 to 32 hours with only a few stops to eat, feed the babies and drug them to sleep again. Eventually, they would arrive in Kuala Lumpur or George Town, where Lam received the babies, paid what was owed and then delivered them to their customers.

Our investigation proved the group also trafficked several young Cambodian women who were promised work as servers in George Town, but instead, were sequestered in a house of prostitution and sexually exploited.

Baang's nets also pulled in several boys from 8 to 10 years old, who were put to begging in Bangkok. This strange system exploited children by placing them at the bottom of staircases in busy metro stations or at shopping center exits. They had to sit on the ground by themselves, two or three in a group, or with a woman holding a baby in her arms, or with a handicapped man. There, they begged for coins from passersby, always keeping an eye out for police officers, ready to run if they spotted one. They would hide an arm or fold a leg to make people believe they'd been maimed by a landmine explosion, a far too common occurrence in the Cambodian countryside, which is strewn with unexploded ordnance. These beggars collected coins from Thais and tourists, and at night they slept with their exploiters in hovels outside the town.

After the Takeo social services department sent information to our unit implicating Baang Maryan in the disappearance of three babies from six to ten months old, we put an end to this unscrupulous trio's trafficking operation.

I still remember Baang's interrogation. She began by denying everything, claiming she had married a Thai man and lived with him in Thailand, but had to return to Cambodia every three months as a visa requirement. The things being said about her in Takeo were false, she said, motivated by jealousy of her life in Bangkok. She pretended she barely knew Lam Thy, the woman she was accused of supplying with children and women. But the police had photos of her meeting with Lam, and they told her Lam was ready to confess in exchange for freedom to leave Cambodia, with no jail time. They said that the things Lam had heard about Cambodian prisons had made her quite docile.

At the same time, Malaysian investigators were pursuing the inquiry in Malaysia, where they discovered Lam belonged to a major human trafficking network. Their police arrested about a dozen people for aiding and abetting human trafficking in Malaysia and Thailand, and the results of this international investigation were shared in information exchanges with INTERPOL in Bangkok, which had a cooperation accord with our special unit.

At the request of the Malaysian judicial authorities, the Cambodian government extradited Lam to Kuala Lumpur, where she was sentenced to eight years in prison. Baang collaborated with the Cambodian judiciary by denouncing the trafficking network, so she was allowed to return to Thailand but forbidden to reenter Cambodia. That turn of affairs bothered me – I would have much rather put her behind bars – but sometimes events are beyond our control and criminals don't get the punishment they deserve.

The police were also able to recover a 19-year-old girl in George Town and restore her to her family in Pailin in the western part of Cambodia. She had been forced into prostitution by the manager of a George Town bar. We were certain that other young Cambodian girls were trapped in the same situation, some being exploited sexually, others voluntarily engaged as sex workers in Thailand, Malaysia and other countries farther away. But we also knew our limits. Despite the Project's excellent results, we could not change the world – all we could do was to investigate the cases brought to our attention.

The Khmer-Malaysian case showed that cooperation with Malaysia could be difficult, even though our mutual aim was to act in the best interests of trafficking victims.

We had requested a meeting with the Malaysian embassy concerning two young Cambodian girls forced into sexual slavery there. Their employer, who had hired them as housecleaners, turned out to be a trafficker. The diplomats' reaction shocked me, no matter how familiar their words were by then: "Those are lies! Those girls are falsely denouncing their employers to get more money from them. We're civilized, religious people."

Before they would even consider the complaint or accept our department chief's report, we had to use all our powers of persuasion, and play back to them the telephones calls for help the two victims had made to their families, pleading for help. Even after the file was transferred to the relevant department in Kuala Lumpur, two months passed before the Cambodian girls made it home. But they did make it home.

Continuing the investigation in Cambodia, we identified a travel agency director who was relaying victims, including these two girls, into Malaysia, but of course she insisted she knew nothing about the roles they would play upon arrival there. She was never brought to court.

Although the Malaysian authorities took action in a few cases of trafficking for sexual exploitation, they more often refused to recognize the full import of the facts, preferring to speak of "misunderstandings," or of some form of "happy polygamy" entered into with the consent of all parties.

And the men buying up these girls? They were found guilty of...absolutely nothing.

Easier work, better pay – and an advance on that pay – were enticements commonly used to convince families to let their children leave home and country. But some trafficking agents possessed an even more powerful secret weapon to persuade young Cambodian country girls to move to a foreign land: marriage.

At that time, most Cambodian marriages were arranged. It sometimes happened that such an agreement corresponded to the heart throbs of the future spouses, but usually it was an affair tied to the economic and "diplomatic" interests of the families. From the highest to the lowest levels of society, it had always been this way. This continues even now – arranged marriages are not considered an aberration. Cambodian society is structured around clans, whose first circle is the family. Thus, to consolidate their power, many members of government, dignitaries, and rich businessmen married their children to the children of members of other clans. A well-matched couple then furthered the development or protection strategies of both their families.

To avoid the risk of losing face if one of the parties should refuse the alliance, the initial approach between the two families usually fell to a matchmaker, most often a woman, who made this type of negotiation her quasi-profession.

Our unit became interested in matchmakers who specialized in marriages between single, divorced, or widowed Khmer men living out of the country and young, pretty Cambodian women with whom they could found a family or remake their life. This kind of intermediary earned good money for her services. When the man arrived in Cambodia – for the marriage had to be celebrated there – the negotiations with the girl's family were already taken care of. The Khmer from the United States or elsewhere then discovered his promised one, having only seen photos of her up to that time.

For the young girl, an enticing perspective opened, that of building a better life for herself while also helping support her family back home. And if after a few years her husband didn't suit her or was abusive or stingy, she figured she could leave him and find another one in her adopted country.

The meeting phase usually went smoothly. Then the traditional ceremony was organized, the husband paid the dowry – *thlay teck dah* – which means "the price of milk," the administrative formalities were taken care of, and the man would fly off with his young bride, the girl with the bronzed face and the marveling, yet sad eyes. Sad at leaving her country, family and friends, even if it was to go discover a new life in a new land. Most people who move to a foreign country feel this conflict. They hope for a better life in an exciting new place but face the pain of separation from their loved ones, from familiar surroundings, from the spice-perfumed foods they might never savor again.

I myself have felt this conflict throughout my career, even though I had a mission I was passionate about, a definite salary, a precise framework, and my safety was assured. It would have been much more difficult leaving my country with an unknown person to build a new life in a strange world, like a "mail-order" Cambodian bride must.

This type of arranged marriage became popular in the 1990s, and it was a natural magnet for traffickers of young girls for sexual purposes. What could be easier than to settle in Cambodia and commence operations behind the front of "matrimonial agency?"

A group of Taiwanese did just that in 1997. They openly sought young girls, preferably virgins, in view of marrying them to Taiwanese men fascinated by the beauty of Khmer women, and the ease in acquiring them. This fake agency hired a team of Cambodians, six women and one man, who crisscrossed the provinces looking for candidates to present to their employers, two to four at a time, then to the Taiwanese clients, whose travel and lodging was provided for, along with a guarantee they would find a suitable young woman.

Once a choice had been made, negotiations began, with an interpreter or in English if the girl was proficient. The agency and its Cambodian associates would have already arranged the material conditions of the candidate's departure, painting an idyllic vision to her parents of a future in which they would receive 800 to 1200 dollars a month, depending on how beautiful the young lady was. All expenses included: passport, visa formalities, medical exams, clothing suitable to the season, etc. The Taiwanese men were generally from the middle class, averaging 35 to 50 years old, and were introduced as having a solid social standing and comfortable means.

There were no statutes regulating this profession in Cambodia, so the agency operated without any oversight for at least three years. They apparently greased the palms of local authorities to get necessary permissions and papers quickly and quietly, and things went so well that about 300 young girls left the country for Taiwan through this channel.

Eventually, the General Department of Immigration and INTERPOL's National Central Bureau of Cambodia special police service became aware of this agency, for several reasons. First, the criteria listed in their advertisements progressively changed from "young, healthy and hard-working woman desiring to become a foreign bride in exchange for a comfortable life," to criteria such as "tall, beautiful woman with long hair and shapely body." As if they sought a model, not a model wife.

Then, the police noticed that certain Taiwanese supposedly looking for a spouse had come back several times, departing with three or four girls each time, saying they also needed a cook and housemaid, or future salesgirls for their businesses. Of course, training for these roles was promised.

Finally, the Cambodian embassy in Taipei began sending reports of complaints from young Khmer women of being forced into prostitution, when they had been promised marriage or a job. These girls had been naive, you might argue, but they had been persuaded by examples of successful marriages, supported by photos that attested to the agency's reputation. They left home because they wanted to believe in a better future in a richer country, and they figured once there, they could always manage to get along.

Did they consider the risk of landing in some bar or brothel? Probably. Still, they thought it was better to take that chance than to endure the hardship and poverty of their lives in Cambodia. The ancient concept of karma also played a role: "If I'm mistreated, I must have done something bad in a former life."

Under the direction of the Deputy Commissioner of Phnom Penh, General Bith Kim Hong, who later became national director of our specialized department, we put together a file on the matrimonial agency employees and the victims' testimonies, and in August 2000, a raid was ordered. The police burst into the agency's office at the Beauty Hotel near the Independence Monument and arrested five Taiwanese citizens and seven Cambodians. They found 20 young women from 18 to 23 years old in rooms there, ready to leave for Taiwan and elsewhere. They all declared they were prepared to go, and all used nearly the same words: "Whatever the work is over there, it'll be better than here."

When a colleague expressed outrage at this sentiment, I replied, "What right have we to censure them? We've had every opportunity to get a good education, to meet a loving spouse, to never know true misery. It's better to say nothing than to judge them from self-righteous morals."

This was our first case of large-scale international human trafficking, but sadly, there were others.

One of the most complex types of trafficking is that of international adoption. This activity appeared in Cambodia in the 1990s under the guise of adoption intermediaries and "bona fide" adoption agencies. Like traffickers in the arranged marriage trade, these criminals unashamedly exploited their targets' cursory education and extreme poverty.

Lauryn Galindo was the most famous and efficient of these adoption entrepreneurs. I met her for the first time at the Hotel Sunway in Phnom Penh, where most international meetings, seminars or appointments with foreign colleagues take place. She thrilled the pretty salesgirl at the souvenir shop by buying nearly two dozen gifts, ranging from ornate jewelry made of Pailin "Pigeon Blood" rubies and sapphires from east Cambodia to fine silks bearing the Artisans Angkor label, and bronze statuettes created by Khmer artists.

Galindo was a flamboyant dresser, often wearing bright red with matching lipstick. Her long blond hair and model's graceful strut guaranteed she would not pass unnoticed in the city. She was usually accompanied by one or two American couples looking like they had just stepped off the plane, perspiring heavily and returning the smiles of the local inhabitants, whose culture they probably knew little of. These couples weren't ordinary tourists, though. They were there to adopt a Cambodian child, having signed a contract with Seattle Adoptions International, the agency Galindo and her sister ran to ease the whole process. Their most famous client was the American actress Angelina Jolie, who adopted a seven-month-old Cambodian baby in 2002 with Galindo's help. Having a client like that improved Galindo's reputation of course and her fortunes.

As a sign of her fortune and power, Galindo rode around in one of the few Mercedes to be found in Cambodia in 1997, with a deferential English chauffeur and a bodyguard in the passenger seat, doubtless a former soldier.

Galindo had been a hula dancer in Hawaii before coming to Phnom Penh to forge her enviable position. She had soon learned how Cambodia functioned. Several times a year, you would see her on television distributing loads of food or donating tons of rice, elbow to elbow with the highest authorities in the country, in particular Chea Sim, the powerful Senate president from 1999 to 2015. Her carefully established relations with the powers-that-be and the generosity she showered to the poor were integral parts of her business strategy.

Her recruiters, mostly female, canvased the country for women who were pregnant or had just given birth. Her ideal targets were adolescents or young women abandoned by their baby's father, and women who already had too many children to support.

Their usual procedure to dupe a pregnant woman was to visit her in the hospital when she was about to give birth, when a woman is at her most vulnerable physically and psychologically, having been deserted by the person who should have been present. The recruiters would provoke her into thinking about her future, exaggerating the gravity of her situation and offering a solution "in the interest of the baby" that would free her from such a heavy responsibility. They would promise to find a place in an orphanage run by an American NGO where her child would be cared for and properly nourished. She could go with her newborn baby to see it for herself and could visit according to the rules fixed by the orphanage. And she could take the child home if and when her situation improved.

The young woman would feel relieved, and a few days later, her infant would be brought to the orphanage, usually in her company, but not always. The intermediary, whose purported mission was "to save poor children," then gave the mother from 80 to 120 dollars, a small fortune for someone like her, in exchange for her signature on a few "admission" forms. She was told the money came from the generous souls who financed the orphanage.

Although many young mothers never visited the orphanage to see their children, those who did, a few weeks or months later, were met with a refusal: "It's not a good time," the receptionist would say. "It would disturb the baby and then there would be the risk of illness."

If the mother created a scene and insisted on getting her child back, the orphanage personnel would demand she first pay back the money she had received, along with an exorbitant fee to defray their expenses. Such a large sum would be extremely difficult to gather – that was part of the strategy of course – and after a few months, it was too late. The child had been spirited away, with a new identity validated by passport and visa.

Sometimes, with the complicity of a staff member, a child was simply kidnapped from the maternity ward, or a sleeping baby was stolen as it lay only yards away from its mother while she worked. These crimes were riskier, as they led to the police being involved, so they didn't occur as frequently. Making an "arrangement" with the mothers was so much easier. How could they file a complaint after voluntarily confiding their babies to a woman working for an NGO? Was it not a golden opportunity for her and her baby?

After recruiters had managed to convince a mother that adoption was the best solution for her child, so he or she would have a good life in America and perhaps even come back for her one day, they would offer to pay her to find other mothers in her entourage, poor and isolated, or in distress because the pregnancy was not wanted, who could also put their babies up for adoption. In this way, consciously or not, the mothers became accomplices of the intermediaries and the network they belonged to.

Money flowed in and out of Galindo's well-oiled system. Village chiefs furnished the civil documents, because at this lowest of all possible bureaucratic levels, they were not only cheap, but drew the least attention. Especially since they were drawn up in villages far from where the mother lived. For a modest compensation and a pat on the back for "acting on behalf of poor children," the chiefs certified the baby had been abandoned and taken to the orphanage, its parents unknown. They usually stated the baby had been left at a pagoda during the night or on a bench close to a hospital – such details gave credibility to the lie. There was always a minimum of information about the child and its origin. Armed with the village chief's certificate, it cost only a bit more money and effort for the Galindo sisters' agency to get an official birth certificate and identity card for the baby.

In this way, the child entered the international adoption market. After a few months in one of the orphanages the two sisters financed, the orphan was tucked into the arms of its new parents, usually from the United States. The American embassy issued visas on the strength of the official documents, signed, stamped and delivered by the local authorities.

The adoptive parents were overjoyed to finally have a child, and as a bonus, to feel they were saving an orphan from a future of misery. All that for only 10,000 dollars. They were pleased with such a low agency fee, and they avoided the arduous process couples from many other countries confronted when trying to adopt. For example, a French couple was obliged to spend at least two months in Cambodia and open their wallets again and again to pay fees in government bureaus. But through Seattle Adoptions International, a couple could choose their baby out of a catalogue sent to their home in the USA, and then merely take a trip to Cambodia to pick up their baby.

So irreproachable on the surface, this enterprise may well have continued to prosper, for the supply of babies seemed as boundless as the demand, except that a local NGO intervened.

Members of the organization LICADHO became concerned about the high number of newborns and infants being adopted, and on analyzing the procedures followed by Seattle Adoptions International, they noted irregularities and abuses, especially the weak or altogether absent monitoring and control mechanisms in the Cambodian phase of adoption, and the ease in getting visas.

Very few complaints had been filed, though, and in the few cases where police recovered children and restored them to their mothers, judges blamed the village chiefs for "administrative errors" and closed the cases.

Our department became aware of the trafficking risks linked to adoption procedures when the hotline started receiving calls denouncing the practice. I got in touch with LICADHO investigators so the police could use their information when looking into reported cases. But adoptions were more in the social services line, and civil registry inquiries fell under the jurisdiction of the Inspector General of Administrative Services. Only confirmed reports of abduction could be considered for criminal investigations by the police, and at that time, September 2001, the matter was considered too complex to move on it.

It was not until several years had passed and Galindo's agency had "delivered" some 800 infants that the immigration authorities finally took action. Pressured by LICADHO and various IOs, they took up the affair. A delicate one, considering Galindo's high-level relationships, the human aspects of the affair, the difficulty of verifying the true status of adopted orphans or uncovering irregularities or infractions committed during the adoption process.

As for the adoptive parents, they had been confident in the agency, the orphanages, and the Cambodian authorities, to the point that not one adoption was cancelled. They had nothing to reproach themselves for.

After a lengthy international investigation by U.S. Immigration and Customs Enforcement, Homeland Security Investigations and the U.S. embassy in Phnom Penh, the two sisters were arrested in Hawaii in 2004 for money laundering, forgery and use of forgery in the aim of facilitating adoptions by fraudulent means. They were each sentenced to 18 months in prison and seizure of all property associated with activities deemed illegal.

Not one charge of human trafficking was leveled against the two sisters.

To whom did they bring happiness, and to whom only wretchedness? All we can say with certainty is that in full knowledge of the facts – for they knew Cambodia – these two women chose to amass a fortune by playing on the economic misery of some and the yearning for a child of others. Worse, they chose profits over the risk of inciting yet more trafficking of infants in the criminal underworld.

IX - The Tiger Takes a Fall

Fifteen years ago, I received the following letter from "Jane," a Canadian woman I had assisted in Cambodia: "I was sitting in the courtroom Monday, waiting for the verdict, and I felt terribly nervous, thinking of all the work people had done to bring my case to this point. When the court's decision came down, I felt incredibly relieved. I immediately thought of you. You were the first person to listen to me and believe in what I wanted to do. I'm proud to have met you, although I'm sorry it had to take place in such awful circumstances. I admire you and the stupendous work you do here. Please take care of yourself, and again, thank you very much."

Police officers aren't looking to be loved or to be feared, but to be respected by the actors in the cases they handle is crucial. So, Jane's letter touched me deeply, and still does. It reassures me, too, because it shows me I've accomplished my duty as a police officer. Coming from a woman who was raped at gunpoint, her words are especially important, a reminder of how victims sometimes must struggle to get their testimony heard – even concerning one of the worst possible crimes – and that no matter what the circumstances, our duty and honor as police officers require us to stand by their side.

Although this case did not have to do with a child, as Jane was 25 when it happened, it occupies an important place in the Project's development and must figure in this book. Another reason to tell her story is to pay tribute to her bravery. Her rapist could have killed her during or after the crime, but Jane returned to Cambodia anyway, to help the police arrest him. She did this despite her trauma and fear, so no other woman could fall into this criminal's hands. And this came at a time when many people thought neither the police nor the Cambodian justice system would raise a finger against him.

It was on April 6, 2004, when her story and ensuing case "interrupted" our unit's agenda. It was only a few days before the Khmer New Year, and a certain inertia had settled into the Ministry of the Interior's offices. Everything would soon be put on hold as employees prepared for the festival days, during which Phnom Penh's residents flowed out of the city until its streets were empty. And at this season, suffocating heat enveloped the capital, discouraging any activity out of range of a fan or air conditioner. It always made me think of how much Phnom Penh residents must have suffered when their city fell on April 17, 1975, and the victorious Khmer Rouge forced them to leave. Pushed into streets sweltering under a leaden sky, they had to keep walking hour after hour for entire days. Many people died in that nightmare of "three years, eight months and twenty days."

It was my habit to reach my office early every morning to read the *Cambodia Daily* and *Cambodge Soir*, the two daily foreign-language papers, before work. That day, a front-page headline in the Daily caught my attention: "Sihanoukville tourists agitated by rapes on beach."

Sexual aggressions against Cambodian women happened frequently, in towns and in the countryside, despite all the information campaigns, social work of various NGOs and progress within the police and judicial system. But this article concerned foreign tourists raped in a seaside resort, one of the principal tourist destinations in the country, second only to the temple of Angkor Wat.

I knew the place well. Ever since my arrival in Cambodia in 1994, I had spent my vacations there, attracted by its tranquility, fine sandy beaches and the fresh seafood in restaurants that popped up on the beaches immediately after the United Nations Blue Berets[25] had arrived in Cambodia.

The article reported that a female tourist had been raped at gunpoint on the night of March 31, and Sihanoukville hotel managers were warning their clients against the dangers of walking alone at night. It also claimed the rapist was a Cambodian man wearing a uniform like that of a policeman. It stated the victim was too shook up to talk about the incident; instead, she had immediately packed her bags and left for her embassy in Phnom Penh. Since she had filed no complaint, the local police considered the assault a rumor, and took no action.

However, the incident did take place, and it had the effect of a lightning bolt tearing apart the resort's postcard-perfect landscape. Normally, a carefree exhilaration reigned in Sihanoukville, where mostly young tourists could lodge at inexpensive hotels and count on equally low-priced drinks and meals. Under generous sunshine or warm tropical showers, the long, nearly deserted beaches invited them outdoors, as did the nights full of the sound of partying. A bit of earthly paradise, illumined by the Khmer residents' marvellous smiles, which delighted travelers fleeing winter in cold gray lands.

This story of rape brutally recalled those tourists back to grim reality, and anyone reading it would think twice about visiting Sihanoukville. Like everywhere else, criminals hid in the shadows in the Realm of Smiles. The disappointment was cruel. Tourists saw those smiles as the expression of infinite bounty, kindness and the joy of life. But in this small country, most people carry a heavy burden of trauma and privation, and the smiles on their serene faces hide worries and wounds, shyness and self-effacement, as if asking pardon for existing.

And sometimes the smile hides a twisted personality full of jealousy and rancor, capable of the worst abominations.

Jane met such a man at the beach on the night of March 31. Her hurried departure, without notifying the police of her assault, suggested what I already knew, that when it comes to a case of rape, especially if the perpetrator wore a uniform, few foreigners, expatriate or tourist, expect much help from the Cambodian police.

We had been assisting the Sihanoukville investigative department for two years and had even set up one of our regional units there, but I learned about this crime from the newspaper rather than from the police hierarchy. As counsellor to the Ministry of the Interior, I could not ignore it, however, especially since the criminal might belong to the same department.

This was a unique occasion for us to take strong measures in the fight against sexual crimes. The victim being a foreigner, I had a compelling argument to pressure the authorities into action: The impact would be catastrophic on tourism if they ignored a rapist and left him to prowl the beaches and streets of Sihanoukville, a resort destination that was starting to win international renown.

I also saw an opportunity to strike a blow against the impunity of men in uniform and the complacency of their superiors, who tended to close their eyes to a man's behavior as long as it didn't work against their own interests. On the contrary, by granting that favor, the erring man became indebted to his superior.

But to strike that blow, I would have to overcome a series of obstacles. First, convince the Chief of Police to open an investigation and let it follow its course – no matter where it led. Then, convince UNICEF to let us take a case that had nothing to do with protecting children, although it did fall within the jurisdiction of the division we had helped create and maintain. And if I accomplished those two things, would the victim even return to Cambodia to file a complaint and work with our investigators? Would the military or police hand over one of its men if we implicated him? Could I keep magistrates and police officers at work in the middle of their traditional New Year festivities to investigate the rape case of a tourist who was no longer even in the country?

I decided to stop counting the obstacles, but to face them head on. I called the Canadian consulate, and a diplomat there confirmed the facts of Jane's case. I assured him that if she came back, we would register her complaint and set an investigation in motion with my full support, regardless of the suspect's rank, role or uniform.

Those words, "with my full support," laid an enormous responsibility on my shoulders, for if she returned, the investigation must not fail to bring her rapist to justice. We would have to return to the scene of the crime to conduct the inquiry – assuming she had the courage. We would have to protect her from her attacker if he tried to silence her. And could we could put him behind bars? I would understand her bowing out, as the consulate had at first advised her. Why take so many risks based on my lofty words alone? Nevertheless, the diplomat promised to contact her as soon as possible.

If she did return, it could be very soon, and on that supposition, I launched into preparations. To start, I needed to get the green light from my immediate supervisors. UNICEF was unwilling at first. In supporting our child protection program within the Ministry of the Interior, this UN organization was already working in unfamiliar territory, and to intervene in a police investigation of the rape of an adult brought it even further afield. However, I was lucky enough to have as my UNICEF contact a woman affected by a close friend's rape, and she listened to me with concern. I explained this affair would advance the police department's handling of sex crimes, and in turn, benefit the struggle against sexual attacks on children. Not only that, but it would test the true determination of local authorities to put sex offenders behind bars.

She listened to me and asked only that I remain behind the front lines.

Next, I needed General Hok Lundy's backing. As Director of National Police, he was a man nobody risked disobeying, as I have mentioned. He lent me his complete support, for he understood Cambodia needed tourism to fuel the economy and couldn't afford to get a reputation for cutthroats and rapists.

The UN assigned me vehicles to travel to the scene of the crime. Once in Sihanoukville, it would fall to me to cope with other dangers: aggression or threats against the victim if she dared to speak out and file a complaint; refusals to cooperate by the suspect's superiors; discovering the criminal was an officer I had trained, among many others. I also had to anticipate hostile reactions from the provincial court and local police, who might fear reprisals, and make sure the officers assigned to the investigation were people I had worked with and trusted. It was also indispensable to have a woman on the team. I needed to organize the victim's travel arrangements, protect her, keep her informed and support her so everything would take place without incident. All that and more, and all from behind the scenes.

On April 8, Jane returned to Cambodia accompanied by her friend Denise, with whom she had shared a room in Sihanoukville. I met Jane that day for the first time. Rather tall, shapely and pretty, cheerful despite her obvious embarrassment at talking about her experience. She told me she worked as a professor in Seoul and had come to Sihanoukville on vacation in March, never imagining she could be attacked in such a peaceful spot.

I asked no questions during this first meeting at the hotel. I wanted to put her at ease, build confidence and comfort her in her decision to file a complaint. I mentioned the meetings we had arranged without touching on details of any eventual trip to Sihanoukville, and I assured her Denise could accompany her everywhere, even to the police station or the scene of the crime. I then suggested she write down everything that had happened to her on the night of March 31 with as many details as possible about the suspect, circumstances, chronology, and places. That way, she could turn in her deposition the following day and formalize the complaint.

Everything had been carefully prepared to receive her in a soothing atmosphere. Appearing before the police and reciting what she had endured was a painful ordeal, but it was the first step in obtaining justice, a crucial step in easing her mind of the anguish of what had happened.

She spoke for a long time, answering questions and detailing what she had written. She had met her rapist a little after midnight on a path used as a shortcut between the beach and the guesthouse she and Denise were staying in. She was heading to a café on the beach, alone. Denise wasn't feeling well that evening, so she had remained in their rooms.

"I'd walked about thirty yards or so when I noticed a man standing in the shadows, a gun in his hand. It looked like an army rifle.

"Suddenly, he stepped out right in front of me. I lifted my hands asking him what he wanted, if he wanted money. He shook his head and made a sign to me to go into a little hut on the right. I waved my hand to show I didn't want to, and I started to back up slowly, but he pointed the gun at me and pointed at the door. His eyes were terrifying. I didn't move, so he started shouting at me. I was shaking all over, but I went in. He came in, leaving the door open, and told me to take off my pants.

"I shook my head and waved my hands again to show I didn't want to do that.

"'Do you want to die?' he asked me. And I could see the black gun pointed at my chest.

"I was wearing mauve-colored cotton pants that tie around the waist. I did what he told me, and there I was, in my underwear in front of this man threatening me with a gun, alone at night. My friends were so close, only about two hundred yards away, but I knew I couldn't shout, or he would panic and shoot me or smash my face with the butt of the gun.

"He told me to take my panties off. They were white with a design in front, like the kind little girls wear. Then he made me lie down, pointing his gun at a long low table that must have been used as a bed.

"Then the endless nightmare began. It seemed as if the man had prepared it all. He raped me with his penis but also his fingers and the tip of his gun. It hurt so bad I couldn't help crying out, but he yelled at me.

"'Don't shout! Why are you shouting?'

"'Because I'm scared,' I said. 'Because I want to go home.'

"He repeated over and over, 'Canada, Canada, Canada,' like it excited him. And he said I knew him. 'No? I've seen you three times. You're a beautiful girl and I like you a lot,' he said.

"When he finally finished, he demanded money from me, and tore my little purse out of my hands. But his hands were shaking so much he couldn't manage to get the bills out.

"He told me to put my clothes back on, then asked me where I was staying. I pointed in the opposite direction from where my room was, but he must not have believed me because he ordered me to go toward my guesthouse. Then he pointed the gun at me again as I was leaving, and said, 'And don't say a word about this to anyone if you want to stay alive!'

"I told him I wouldn't say anything, and without another word, I took off into the dark."

In the description she gave of her attacker, Jane did not mention a uniform. We understood later that this "information" reported in the press came from the fact that people in the area knew the hut where the rape had taken place belonged to a gendarmerie garrison. The criminal bore a military weapon, so they deduced he must be a gendarme[26] or police officer stationed in the area, a deduction echoed by the journalists.

After getting back to the guesthouse that night, where everyone was shocked at hearing what had happened, Jane contacted the Canadian embassy in Phnom Penh. They told her to come as soon as possible.

"You can see a doctor here and then get out of the country. It's useless to file a complaint here – it won't go anywhere," the embassy representative said.

Frightened that the man would regret having released her and might try to find her and kill her, Jane left Sihanoukville very early the next morning, April 1.

"When I got to the embassy, the people there immediately took me under their wing. They brought me to a doctor, who examined me and collected samples. I didn't have any visible injuries except bruises from hitting the table and signs of vaginal irritation. The doctor gave me some medicine, a 'morning-after' pill, and another pill to lower the risk of HIV infection. That very afternoon, Denise and I took off for Bangkok, and two days later, we went to Koh Samui, where some friends were staying. I wanted to clear my head. But after one night there, I realized I couldn't just go home and ignore the crime I'd been a victim of. And I thought about all the girls that creep could rape if I said nothing. I felt obligated to act.

"I phoned the man who had helped me at the embassy, to share what I felt with him, that I was torn between my duty to denounce that criminal and fear of putting myself in danger. After several calls and communications, I received an email saying that Monsieur Christian Guth, a consultant to the Cambodian police, was ready to help me if I wanted to return to Cambodia and file a complaint. That reassured me, and I made my decision right then."

On reviewing her deposition and formal complaint, I imagined "justice" as an invisible thread being woven into a web to catch this criminal, who was probably feeling secure in the knowledge the "white girl" would keep quiet. But in the great book of karma, it was written otherwise, and Jane, an altruistic, brave woman, and I, a man revolted by impunity, would unite to bring him to justice.

Her friend Denise made an important addition to the deposition by emphasizing their state of panic on that April day as they waited for the bus that would "evacuate" them to Phnom Penh. Jane had told her that just after the rape, the man said he had noticed her on the beach and "hoped she had enjoyed herself, so it would be a shared experience."

It is common for rapists to take refuge in denial after the act and try to extract some form of consent from their victim. But that pitiful escape route would not work in the present case – his brandishing a semi-automatic rifle would condemn him to a maximum sentence.

But only if we caught him.

So, to advance the investigation, we organized a trip to the scene of the crime to reconstitute the victim's steps and physically validate her statement. The rapist was still free – would he have remained in the area? We had to be careful not to awaken his suspicions, to let him go on thinking he was scot-free in the hopes he would stay quiet while the investigation progressed. And if he did catch on to us, how would he react? Would he be seized with that well-known murderous fury and "run amok" while in possession of a deadly weapon?

Our movements had to be rapid, discreet and timed down to the last second. With a detailed plan in hand and General Hok Lundy's support, I had no difficulty in getting my instructions obeyed. At 9:00 am, our convoy of two 4WD cars pulled into the courtyard of the provincial police chief's office for a "courtesy visit," but mainly to get confirmation from his own lips that there would be no police wearing uniforms or openly carrying guns along our course. He furnished us with an escort of plain-clothes officers with concealed guns. A few minutes later, we were walking down the road to the beach. Jane seemed emotional, anxious, but her friend was holding her hand and we spoke to her calmly to reassure her.

"Jane, we're going to walk slowly to the beach and then to the café where you usually went in the evening. On the way back, we'll take the same path you did that night, alright?"

At the café, a few customers sat at tables under an awning or reclined on rattan chairs sipping fruit juice. It was hard not to attract attention, but luckily the beach was uncrowded at that early hour.

The owner recognized Jane and greeted her warmly, then started talking about the rumors circulating in the little seaside community. People in every small town seem to like showing they know more than anyone else, and he claimed the men behind the recent rapes (for we'd learned there had been other cases besides Jane's, whose victims had left the country rather than file a complaint) were men enshrouded in impunity, "tools for the ruling powers, whom nobody could arrest or even accuse."

We would see about that.

We then headed to the shortcut leading to the guesthouse. Following Jane and Denise, we followed the curve of the beach about 200 yards to another beach café, then turned left onto a path traced in the sand. There was no one in the area, in accordance with my agreement with the gendarmerie squadron commander. The only noise we heard was the swishing of our feet in the sand – no wind, no birds calling. We wore hats to hide our features, and big drops of perspiration rolled down our faces and necks. Was the suspect watching us? I would never know, but each step counted as a relief. After 30 or 40 such steps, Jane showed us the spot where the armed man had stood on the night of March 31. Then we saw the hut. The door was open, and no one was there. Inside was a kind of table or bed made of wood slats. Jane gestured at it; that was where she had been raped.

Her friend pulled her into a hug. Jane was deeply moved, her face grave. Fear showed in her eyes, but also a glow of anger that shouted: "That bastard has to pay for what he did to me!"

I wondered what the rapist's reaction would have been if he had come by and recognized Jane, despite her hat? It was a risk we had to take. Covering this ground with Jane was important to show we weren't afraid of him, and also to examine the crime scene, where, in the middle of the night, walking in the still-warm sand, she had found herself all alone, abandoned to the savagery of that man. Suddenly, she said she knew he could have killed her, and she started shivering violently. Terrible images were coming back to her mind. The man's cruel features, his eyes, his gun, his arm raised against her, her body violated, the fear of never seeing her friends or family again.

One of the policemen photographed the area. They had been documenting our entire course since arriving in the parking lot. We checked for objects in the hut, but there was nothing, no other furniture except for a wooden chair planted in the sand outside the entrance.

Finally, just before noon, it was over. My colleagues went to interrogate the hostess of the guesthouse. But even if she had known the rape suspect, she wouldn't have talked. It was simply too dangerous. The rest of us left for the opposite side of the seaside town, past Ochheuteal beach, and stopped at a restaurant shaded by giant eucalyptus trees. We took seats on the terrace and had a quiet lunch together. Fish grilled with *ambel, mrek, krouchma* – salt, pepper, and lemon juice – and rice of course. One of my favorite dishes, and one I knew pleases most everyone in any circumstances. Jane was still anxious, but

I felt she was relieved too. She knew she had made the right decision; she had gathered her courage and returned to Cambodia to face her fears, and whether the man was arrested and judged guilty or not, she had done her part. Now it was time for him to shake in his boots.

Back in Phnom Penh, General Un Sokunthea, who was supervising the investigation, told us the Sihanoukville police had all the elements they needed to identify the criminal. Jane and Denise were to fly home the next day. There was no guarantee the rapist would be arrested, judged and sentenced any time soon, as the country was about to start the New Year week of banquets and reunions. The rumblings we had managed to stir up among the police corps might or might not continue. Now that the first steps in the investigation had been taken, and the victim left Cambodia, the case could fall into oblivion. The authorities had shown their good intentions and glossed over any international concern, so now they could let things be or even help the suspect escape if that seemed more expedient.

And yet, nothing could be easier than to find him. It sufficed to find out who was on duty that night, or near the scene of the crime, then show their photos to the victim. The cooperation the gendarmerie chief had shown thus far would have to be followed up by action, by a firm commitment to arrest the suspect no matter what his function or rank, or who his backers were.

But for now, like the Canadian diplomats, I could do nothing more except to put pressure on the Cambodian police by maintaining my focus on the case. I was determined to reject insidious questions put by those trying to minimize the rapist's culpability, such as, "After all, by taking a lonely path at night, didn't the victim look for what happened to her?"

My invariable response was, "Look at the Penal Code and you'll see rape is a crime. To impose any sexual relationship is a crime, especially penetration at gunpoint. And the international community is monitoring how this plays out. New Year's or not, we need to find this guy."

In Sihanoukville, certain local authorities were trying to muddle the inquiry.

"No one was on guard that night in that area," one man offered up as a diversion. "The suspect could have been a soldier, even a former Khmer Rouge who had kept his gun, and not a gendarme at all."

But then I got a call from an officer I had trained and often talked with. He said that before our visit there with Jane, an armed man had threatened every person who had helped her after the rape. That meant the witnesses we questioned had lied to us. They knew the criminal's identity. But who could blame them, living in a remote spot with an armed, perhaps desperate brute running loose?

I wouldn't give up while the trail was still warm. It could lead us to the criminal, and in the end, it did. Less than two weeks later, General Un Sokunthea informed me a suspect had been identified, a gendarme low in rank but nephew of a *niek thom*, an "important man." This gendarme's nickname was "Khlâ" or "The Tiger," and he was known for his relentless, sometimes violent sexual behavior.

"Whatever he desires, he takes," the general said. "If it's really him, I'm certain this is not his first rape."

My police contact in Sihanoukville told me the man had recently invited his superiors to dinner. It was obvious he was trying to gather their support, convinced that his family and hierarchy connections would grant him immunity from any prosecution.

"For the moment, we're letting him think he's protected," the General continued. "We have to keep absolute secrecy about all of this, so we'll say nothing to the local police for now. Otherwise, the risk is too great he'll flee."

She showed me a photo of the suspect, which his wife had sent. Childish features, wavy hair, superficial smile, non-descript clothes. I emailed the picture to Jane, and she wrote back immediately: "Yes, that's him. He wasn't wearing a shirt or smiling like in this photo, plus his hair was shorter, but I recognize him. Did he escape? Will he be arrested? My thanks to everyone regardless."

The victim having confirmed the suspect's identity, the prosecutor issued a warrant for his arrest, evidently having received instructions from his supervisors. With the gendarmerie chief's agreement, the police arrested the Tiger and found Jane's pocketbook in his possession, containing two photos of Jane and cash exactly matching the amount and currencies she had declared, so we assumed it was her money.

The Tiger turned out to be a man named Khun Thorn, from Svay Rieng, a mostly poor province in western Cambodia. The local police interrogated him, and he admitted having sexual relations with a young Western tourist during the night of March 31 – April 1, but he claimed she was a consenting partner.

"I kept noticing her because she and her friend took the path to the beach by the garrison post, that unoccupied hut, several days in a row," he said. "I liked her looks. That night she was alone. I speak a little English, so I stopped her and asked her for some money. When she just kept walking, I blocked her way and made her go into the hut nearby. She didn't resist at all, so I thought she was okay with it. I didn't hit her or hurt her, and she gave me her coin purse as a gift."

Our suspect wanted us to swallow a story like that. Films and TV shows often suggest a little violence or domination can lead to a passionate sexual relationship where consent reposes on love, a search for pleasure, a reward. Long debates are held concerning special cases wavering on a fine line between freely given consent and "caving in" to pressures a victim can't overcome. Only a judge can decide. But if consent is absent, it's a case of rape, no matter what means are used.

Never for a moment had this gendarme imagined his hierarchy would fail him and deliver him to the police. His version of the facts as "a love adventure" did not hold up for long. He ended up admitting he had threatened the young tourist with a gun and raped her. When asked why he raped her, he said it was because he'd desired her for several days and he wanted her. That was all.

The prosecutor immediately jailed him to avoid any incidents and to get him away from curious journalists. The arrest of a gendarme there was a first, a sensational bit of news. The country's principal newspaper, *Rasmey Kampuchea*, close to high governmental circles, criticized the fact a young gendarme was thrown in jail on one woman's "allegations." One of their journalists wrote the following:

"In Cambodia, a man can very easily be considered a criminal upon the simple allegations of a woman or young girl. That means men and male teens face heavy legal pressure concerning relations between the two sexes in our society, of which discrimination against men could result [...] Even if he did confess, we don't know with certitude what made him say he had raped the complainant. Who knows?"

This was an implication to cases in Cambodia where the true criminal paid some poor guy in serious debt, abandoned by all, to confess in his place to a crime he did not commit. But in the present case, no doubt could be admitted, and the journalist was reasoning on a postulate as dishonest as it was dangerous in terms of the law: the word of a rape victim is worth nothing.

Unlike the *Rasmey Kampuchea*, another newspaper, the *Borei Thmey Daily*, did not put the conclusions of the investigation into doubt: "The rapes of foreigners coming to visit our country, like in the case that occurred in Sihanoukville, are a disgrace to Cambodia. Foreign tourists bring many benefits to our nation, and the authorities must guarantee their safety against those who commit shameful acts."

We notified Jane of her attacker's arrest and confession, of his expulsion from the gendarmerie and imprisonment, and she identified him again, formally, from photos the police took. She was asked to come back for the trial, which would proceed soon afterward.

The verdict, handed down on September 15, 2004, made the front pages of all the local papers: "Rapist of Canadian tourist sentenced to 15 years in prison."

The *Cambodge Soir* reported: "Even though the suspect retracted his confession before the judges, the evidence against him was sufficient. The defense lawyers tried to plead their client was psychologically frail, but the judge's personal conviction was established."

The paper also cited a police official: "This judgment helps the reputation of our country. It's the first time such a decision was rendered, and it will contribute to strengthen foreigners' confidence in our judicial system."

Interviewed by the *Cambodia Daily*, Jane said she was extremely satisfied with how she was treated by the courts and the police. And of course, I felt enormous satisfaction when the judge announced this unprecedented verdict. I had voluntarily marched into a minefield for a payoff that was far from certain and came through not only unscathed, but with an incredible victory over impunity. The Cambodian police and judiciary would also accord greater importance to sexual crimes from then on.

Above all, justice had been done to Jane.

X - "Junge, komm bald wieder"

Strangely enough, a German song by Freddy Quinn would take on a special role in my mission in Cambodia. "Junge, komm bald wieder," a song that recalled my boyhood days in Alsace. It led to a stronger, more effective partnership between our team at the Ministry of the Interior and the German federal investigative police, or Bundeskriminalamt, abbreviated BKA.

And it led to a life-long friendship with a BKA staff member, Ulrich Schiffer, who operated out of Bangkok. The BKA sent him to Cambodia at the beginning of the dry season in 2002 to follow a lead our unit in Siem Reap had sent to their regional office: We had spotted a 42-year-old pedophile by the name of Karl Jansai, a German wanted by the BKA.

I regularly received visits from European and American colleagues based in Bangkok and Hanoi to catch up on cases involving citizens from our respective countries. Although criminal law is usually territorial, meaning suspects are tried in the country in which the crime was committed, for sex crimes against minors, several nations have adopted "extraterritoriality laws" so that the person accused of a crime or offense is judged in his or her native country. So instead of appearing before a Cambodian judge, with whom the defendants could hope to make an "arrangement," sexual assault suspects can be extradited and placed under their own country's jurisdiction, generally far less tender with pedocriminals abusing children in foreign countries.

With Americans, for example, this process quickly became the norm after the Cambodian authorities concluded an extradition deal with them. As soon as we arrested one of their citizens, federal police arrived to bring him or her back to the United States with the entire case file in hand. For our unit, the affair was terminated. This could be frustrating, for we rarely learned how these cases turned out, but at least we knew the aggressors, if found guilty, would pay dearly in the American judicial system. Unless of course they had the means to hire a top-flight legal team, and then the outcome was more doubtful.

This extraterritorial protocol left little margin for human relationships, let alone friendships, to develop among law enforcement staff of different countries. But this proved different with colleagues in the BKA – and it was thanks to that Freddy Quinn song.

The BKA had contacted me with details on Schiffer's arrival, and I met him at the Phnom Penh airport. I wanted to get acquainted with him and brief him on the situation before heading downtown. I invited him for coffee. Although I had exchanged a few words with Schiffer on the phone, he was surprised to hear me embark directly in his native tongue at our first in-person meeting. Foreigners normally used English to communicate. But as I had grown up in Alsace, a region in north-eastern France that borders Germany and Switzerland, German was my second native language. I could almost hear Schiffer thinking, "We're going to get along well, colleague," as he peered at me with a little smile.

I told him I had little occasion to use German in Cambodia but had once met with a Cambodian prosecutor without my interpreter, and on a whim, had tried a phrase in German. He'd understood! He had studied in East Germany in the 80s, when Cambodia received support only from "brother countries" like the Soviet Union. We both chuckled at the irony, and the ice broken, we started talking about various criminal cases. I recalled a particularly frustrating one concerning a German pedocriminal.

"It was about two years ago. This young man, a 28-year-old, was arrested with a boy of 13 in his hotel room. He managed to flee the country without spending one day in prison, or even going before a judge. And yet, three other victims had been identified and confirmed that the man had paid five to ten dollars to have sex with them."

"Yes, I saw that file," Ulrich said. "He's the heir to a very rich family, and they handle all his affairs, which turned out lucky for him. The other three kids ranged from 11 to 14 years old. They all took cash payments to withdraw their complaints, and the guy instantly ran, before the German embassy or the BKA was even informed."

I sighed and shook my head. "I told a diplomat once how annoying that kind of 'arrangement' is, and how often it occurs in sexual abuse cases. The man just shrugged and said, 'That's Cambodia.' And sure enough, a man from the UK and another from Switzerland did the same kind of disappearing act the following year. The British fellow was arrested for sexual relations with a little girl, and about a month later, the Swiss was brought in for sexually abusing a boy of 14. He managed to bribe his jailers just as he was being remanded into custody, and he left the country that very night. It took a little more time for the Englishman to get out of trouble, but his family eventually paid the girl's parents about 800 dollars to withdraw their complaint and then they bribed the judge handling the case and the man's guards. Given what these people here earn, how could they refuse? And this kind of thing still happens from time to time, but things are changing."

"I hope you're right," Ulrich said.

We left the café to drive to town, and as we headed out of the parking lot, the German song "Junge, komm bald wieder" started blasting on my CD player. Ulrich broke into laughter.

"What's this music? You listen to Freddy Quinn as you drive? That's nuts – it's as old as our grandmothers."

It was indeed Freddy Quinn, singing in his rich tenor a melody sad enough to make a stone cry, about a mother whose son sails the oceans. She begs him to come home and never go to sea again. It dates from 1963, so hearing it in 2002 in a Frenchman's car in Cambodia split his sides. From that moment, a friendly sympathy arose not just between Ulrich Schiffer and me, but with the entire BKA, as I would find out later.

Our friendship deepened even more thanks to our success in the case he'd been assigned to deal with here, concerning the German pedocriminal Karl Jansai. Our unit had tracked him down at the Angkor Wat temple near Siem Reap.

Local police there had accused him of having sexual relations with two girls, 13 and 14 years old. LICADHO recorded the girls' preliminary statements and sent them to our local unit chief in Siem Reap. The police arrested the suspect and he admitted to the facts but kept claiming he thought they were prostitutes over the age of 18. The same refrain as all the others. But our investigation revealed he had visited Cambodia two other times during the last six months and had abused other under-age girls, whom we identified. The police soon possessed their statements too.

The Angkor Wat temples served as Jansai's hunting grounds. He targeted the many children selling souvenirs and soft drinks by offering them gifts of money or sweets. Then he accompanied them to their homes, showering gifts on their parents to gain their trust. Not suspecting he meant evil, they must have thought he liked their children as if they were his own. Jansai presented a sober, reassuring look with his dark, well-fitted clothes and glasses. Plus, he knew a few Khmer words, which is perceived as showing sincere interest in their country and its inhabitants.

When he asked if he could invite the kids to his hotel to hang out together eating fresh fruit and having their pictures taken, the families had no misgivings. But once in his room, he gave the little girls soda containing Clonazepam, a substance popular with sexual delinquents, and then he abused them. The man was a child rapist of the worst sort.

A search of his room revealed three boxes of Clonazepam, two cameras, a video camera, a computer, and memory cards containing hundreds of photos of naked girls, some showing him having sex with minors, sometimes using dildos. For many pedocriminals, photos and videos are like trophies they can exhibit and sell on special networks.

"All of this is being analyzed, and a doctor in Siem Reap has examined the victims," Ulrich told me before heading there. "The captain in charge of the case was one of my best interns, and she's particularly efficient. It can't go wrong."

And it did not: Jansai was extradited to Germany and the courts there sentenced him to 12 years in prison.

The night before Ulrich's return to Bangkok, we dined at a riverside bistro, where I had him taste fish *amok*, the Khmer specialty I love. The fish filet is cooked in coconut cream with mild but flavorful spices and served in a coconut husk or neatly rolled banana leaf. Ulrich did great honor to the delicacy and to the local Anchor beer, and the empty cans started to spill over the trash can placed under the table for that purpose.

The smooth river at our feet under the starry sky, the humming of the fan, the beer diluted in a bock of ice cubes, the smiles of the servers assigned to our table, who made sure our glasses were always filled to the brim – it suddenly felt surreal, this short break from our daily lives spent trudging through the filthy mud of human perversion. After commenting on this, our conversation drifted from subject to subject, light ones, like the foam in our glasses. At one point, Ulrich teased me about the Khmer scarf wrapped around my neck.

"Are you settling in or what?"

Since moving to Cambodia, I was rarely without my *krama*, a long rectangle of cotton or silk, usually in a black-and-white check pattern. The quintessential Khmer accessory, worn from morning til night: on the head and face to protect you from sunshine, cold, wind or dust; as a towel to sponge your forehead; to dry off after bathing or a swim; around your hips, knotted like a pareo; spread on the ground or a bed as a sheet; rolled up on your head to carry trays of merchandise; knotted into a bindle and carried over your shoulder. Towel, scarf, pareo, pouch, sheet – the krama serves every purpose. But there's even more to it.

"You see, Ulrich, this bit of fabric possesses the ability to identify its wearer," I explained. "This one indicates the person lives in Cambodia or has been there. In Thailand, I've heard people say, 'Ah, you prefer the Khmer,' as if by wearing a krama I was rooting for Cambodia, expressing a preference or affection for their people..."

"That's what I was saying, Christian. You're putting down roots."

"Not as much as you think. Do you know, whenever I drive to Sisophon from Battambang, I always stop at this one cheap roadside diner that serves – you're not going to believe this – the best French fries in the world."

Schiffer exploded into laughter, then said, "You only catch a fever in that kind of dodgy place. Those aren't fries they're serving, but monkey bananas fried in old motor oil!"

"I'm not kidding," I said. "A plate of incredibly good fries with thin strips of beef dipped in a mix of salt, pepper and lemon and grilled on a wood fire. The best fries in the world, I tell you, right on the side of a dusty road. It's a tiny place with wooden tables and chairs, facing a knoll topped with an enormous rock. I call it 'Chez Alex,' after the name of the friend from UNICEF who first took me there."

"I get it. When I go back to Bangkok, I'll tell my colleagues that Christian from Phnom Penh is a guy into krama with a side order of fries!"

Ulrich was curious about this outlandish world I operated in, where treachery and dangers of all kinds existed elbow to elbow with comical dysfunction and the improbable. I explained that as an expatriate, I was not always welcome. I got a lot of dirty looks in the local bars, for example, where men in full midlife crisis drink like fish then tour the dance halls to pay young girls so much a minute to bill and coo at them.

"Hey, it's the pedophile hunter!" the boss would call out when I walked in, as much to tease me as to warn his customers not to brag about their exploits with a "little one." For them, I was a nuisance, a sourpuss, "the retired cop who re-enlisted so he can look like a hero again." Or worse, the guy who might handcuff them without blinking an eye if their partying got out of hand.

"Yes, this is a small place, and people get to know your face," Ulrich said. "Not like Bangkok, where you get lost in the crowd."

"Exactly. It's so small you can run across anyone. Like one night in Sisophon, when I ran into our Minister of Status of Women and spent two hours chatting in the hall outside her hotel room."

"Really?"

"Really. You see, she's really motivated about our project and gives us a lot of support, and she wanted to see firsthand the police department's progress in women's affairs. I was there on my regular tour of the provinces, when I check up on ongoing cases. There was only one decent hotel and our rooms happened to be on the same floor. That evening, we'd been talking shop before going upstairs to our rooms. But when she tried to open her door, her key broke in the lock, and it took two hours to get a locksmith to fix it. So, I spent all that time in the hallway making conversation with the minister as the mosquitoes attacked us."

"You French people – you're so delightful!" Ulrich crowed as he grabbed another beer "for the road."

"The funniest part of all is that a centipede about ten inches long had gotten cozy in my sheets when I was out, and if I hadn't been so wide awake thanks to our unexpected chat, I wouldn't have seen it, and it would have bitten my head off."

"The mysteries of karma are impenetrable, my friend."

The next day in the airport lounge, Ulrich bid me goodbye by singing a few lines from "Junge komm bald wieder." And whenever a German citizen or German-speaking person was implicated in a crime, we met up or spoke by phone. We remain in contact. With so much in common, and having lived through such intense experiences fighting crime together, we had become real friends.

Three years later, Ulrich Schiffer's successor at the BKA in Bangkok, Uwe Jansen, sang those same lyrics to me at the start of our first conversation. Freddy Quinn's song seemed to have become a sort of fraternal handshake, an acknowledgment of French-German police cooperation in Southeast Asia. Jansen had called me about a new affair implicating some German citizens.

Working on this case together, we succeeded in dismantling the main production and distribution network of child pornography in Cambodia.

In 2005, a group of five men, all in their 60s, disembarked at Pochentong Airport. While inching their way through the dense crowd to get visas, then to get them stamped, they couldn't have missed seeing the video playing on the television screens scattered around the airport. Our unit had created it with the help of the tourism minister and an NGO partner on the Project. Its goal was to warn sex tourists, wherever they came from, about the risks they would be exposed to if they abused minors. This message also addressed Cambodians in transit through Pochentong, for they too engaged in sexual relations with minors, exploited them through prostitution networks, or helped arrange rendezvous between clients and minors. They needed to grasp that our department was interested not only in foreigners but locals too. They would risk as aggressive a judicial pursuit as any foreign tourist.

The video opened with images of Angkor Wat and Phnom Penh, then of smiling children. The message "Welcome to Cambodia" closes this intro, then the screen turns blueish, and you glimpse a man accompanied by an obviously young adolescent entering a hotel. A text in five languages scrolls: "If you abuse a child, you will ruin his or her life. But you will ruin yours too." A cross-fade shows a hand dialing the police hotline phone number.

Did these five Germans treat this message lightly, or even laugh at it? If so, they were wrong, for what happened to them was exactly as promised. Someone denounced two of them a few weeks after their arrival, proof that our campaign to raise awareness among Cambodians and tourists was starting to work. The three others were not seen again with these two, nor did they attract police attention.

The hotline tip had come from a teacher living near Vat Phnom to the north of the capital. He told his cousin, a police officer, that he kept seeing young adolescents going in and out of a nearby shophouse where two older foreigners had been living for several months. Apparently, they weren't regular tourists, but rented an apartment by the year and made frequent short trips, probably to get new visas in Thailand.

The officer reported this to a colleague in the special AHTJP service[27] at the Phnom Penh commissary, and they set up surveillance.

The shophouses around there were all similar. Two stories, protected by metal gates affixed to the housefronts by a sort of carport or court roofed with sheet metal. This shophouse had a balcony with plants on it. Our surveillance team photographed the two occupants on the first evening. Both in their 60s, one was balding, tall, wearing a striped shirt, gray pants and sandals; the other was completely bald, of medium-height and much heavier, and wore black.

Leaving alone at nightfall, around 7 pm, they walked toward Vat Phnom, chatting calmly. Two hours later, they were seen returning in high spirits, accompanied by four girls about 13 or 14 years old. The investigator on surveillance duty sat nonchalantly on his motorcycle, wearing civilian clothes and a military cap, and looking like the thousands of other moto-dops in the streets of the capital. When he saw the men with the girls, he notified his chief, who soon arrived with four other men in the back of his own truck. (Since service cars are rare, police often use their family car, the same one that transports vegetables to the wife's market stall every morning. The uniform and rank may confer prestige and power to police officers, but as their salary is barely 150 dollars a month, it's usually the wife who pays the bills.)

The chief looked at the photos taken by his subordinates. There was no doubt. The girls, one Vietnamese and the others Khmer, were underage. He had already called the prosecutor, and even though it was 8:30 at night, he ordered an immediate intervention, judging the minors to be in danger even though they were probably prostitutes.

Of the six officers now onsite, two remained in front of the gate to keep an eye on the balcony, and the chief and the three others banged on the front door.

"Police, open up!"

A man, the heavier one, his waist belted with a krama like a countryman, opened the door with a forced smile on his lips. His face fell – he knew the party was over.

"What is it?"

"Sir, we would like to speak with the four children in there with you. Allow me."

Without waiting for a response, three officers pushed into the house, while the fourth remained with the suspect outside the door. They checked all the ground-floor rooms: kitchen, bike storage area, various nooks and crannies. Nobody.

They took the steep staircase up to the second floor and found a place that looked like the scene of an orgy, with soft lighting, a coffee table and two sofas facing each other, a wicker table with soft drinks, beer, fruit and plates of food, half-eaten. Seeing the police, four naked girls hastily slipped on kramas or towels. The man with them, wearing loose shorts, leaped toward the French doors giving onto the balcony, threw himself over the balustrade and fell about 16 or so feet to the ground. They heard a heavy thud as he hit, then his screams of pain. The two officers in front of the house rushed over and held him down until they realized he couldn't walk, so, after bundling him into the chief's truck, they headed to the hospital. In Cambodia, there is no 911, and the chief's truck now had to serve as ambulance.

A search of the house turned up two video cameras, a computer, basic lighting equipment, a few dozen child pornography films, a variety of costumes for the "actresses," whips, dildos, condoms, massage oils, etc.

One of the officers requested another car to take the girls to the station, where an NGO agency had a staff member waiting to help them after their first interviews. Thanks to their statements and the videos, a third German tourist was identified, a little younger than the first two. Caught on film completely nude, his face in full view, he was "having fun" in his own words, with two girls, a 12-year-old and a 13-year-old. The theme of the film was "A great time can be had in Cambodia," promoting it as a paradise for retired aficionados of young girls, and at a low cost. For each video shoot, the girls earned 30 dollars, 10 of which they had to turn over to their pimps. Some scenes included sadomasochist acts that must have been especially traumatic for the young victims.

The police arrested this third man the following day in his home. Three very young Vietnamese boys were there, and when one of these boys admitted he regularly "supplied" the Germans with young girls, the case abruptly took on magnitude. A few days later, my colleagues arrested two more men thanks to data gleaned from one of the girls' cell phones. A quick search of the bars and "beer gardens[28]" in the city sufficed to find them: a Japanese man with child pornography in his possession sitting in a bar-restaurant on rue Pasteur and an Australian in a beer garden in the market square.

Uwe Jansen at the BKA called me to ask if I would take his compatriots in charge. Along with several other countries, Germany helps the Cambodian police with information about suspects' backgrounds, links to other crimes in the region, and interrogations when the person spoke no English, among other things.

The man who had jumped off the balcony spent a week in the hospital and then confessed during questioning, not without trying to minimize the charges leveled against him, blaming his friend, and claiming he didn't know the girls were minors. The same old litany.

The following day he was brought before his embassy's representative, a stern-looking woman. It was pathetic to see how he tried to excuse himself, his face turning red as he babbled away in German that the police had set him up. He obviously assumed I didn't understand his language.

This was the first online child pornography ring the Phnom Penh police brought down. A lengthy investigation by liaison officers based in Bangkok led to people buying these videos in many other countries, and INTERPOL put steps into motion to neutralize them. Searches were conducted and several people were arrested.

At this stage, our Project was no longer directly involved, but we had helped strengthen ties between these liaison officers and the Cambodian authorities, with the goal to shut down such pedophile rings. This commerce, which was then starting to thrive in Cambodia, had been the subject of an alert announced at the Yokohama International Conference in 2001: the fast—developing internet was opening a huge market for the sale of pornographic films featuring minors and inciting pedophiles to come to countries like Cambodia.

Years later, in 2010, the AHTJP conducted a full-scale investigation in cooperation with the French police and brought down a large prostitution network. A French-Cambodian expatriate living in Cambodia had created an online travel guide for sex tourists, promoting Cambodia as a dream destination for adults wanting to enjoy "all" the pleasures in life. The French services identified the website, and my colleague and friend Silvio Courbet offered his expertise to General Bith Kim Hong, successor to Un Sokunthea, to help root it out.

Using a pseudonym, Courbet began communicating with the Cambodian contact, who, like any ordinary travel agent, booked a complete package for him: airport pickup, lodgings, young girls. Once the arrangements were made, one of our men, an old hand at this kind of thing, pretended to be the client. The "local guide," who went by the name of Mey Sovan, greeted our agent at the airport, all smiles, put a jasmine lei around his neck and drove him to a pleasant, discreet apartment near the riverbank and its many restaurants.

Mey had promised to bring him some of those young girls that same evening. He did not realize everything was being filmed from the minute he pulled up at the airport, or that his client was an actor playing the part Courbet and our unit had prepared for him.

This operation was of a more sophisticated nature than most, and it led to the arrests of a Vietnamese woman who pimped teenagers, her intermediary, and a client who had arrived the previous day, an American in search of his prey of predilection: young virgins. Placed under surveillance, he was caught in his hotel room in flagrante delicto with two girls aged 13 and 14.

By analyzing Mey's computer, we learned the site had been active for more than five years, and we were able to identify a few dozen men who had bought the "package tour." The National Central Bureau of INTERPOL was brought in at that point and the investigation took on an international dimension.

This case helped the Cambodian police move up a notch in the fight against cross-border pedophilia. It also strengthened international cooperation in the struggle against sexual exploitation, an aspect of the Project that led me to participate in seminars worldwide as an expert not only in the Cambodian effort but in those of the entire region, since so many of our cases interlaced with cases in other Asian countries. Trips to Bangkok three or four times a year became part of my regular work schedule from that time on.

Over a decade later, I'm still mulling over my mission, and I realize that without the Project, many pedocriminal investigations would have failed due to being geographically limited – they could only take proceed in the country where the crime was committed. But by cooperating with other countries in the region and throughout the world we got indictments and judgments for some of these pedocriminals and put them behind bars. Right where they belong. And then that German song by Freddy Quinn always lilts through my mind.

But whenever I happen to hear the song on the radio or TV, I also think of something my mother said at the end of her life.

It was in 2005, and the Project was bubbling with activity when I received a call from my family. Mother was extremely ill. I was on the point of leaving for Bangkok for one of my seminars, but I told my colleagues I had to fly to France instead. When I finally made it to the hospital, she was very weak and about to be put on life support, but she recognized me.

"Why did you come from so far away and abandon your work?" she said. "You didn't need to do that. I'm just fine."

We talked for five minutes, then she sank into unconsciousness. The next day, she did not recognize me. Her illness was at the terminal stage, and she could die next day or in two weeks or two months... I didn't know what to do. I had to get back, as I had a heavy load of cases and a lot of work scheduled for that month. After a long talk with my sons, I decided to return to Cambodia.

Two days later, I was at the Mulhouse-Bâle airport, feeling strangely nervous. While withdrawing cash from an ATM, I punched in my code three times incorrectly, and bam, lost my credit card. I cursed myself, but I had a few dollars, so I figured I would be alright. As I entered the boarding area, I got the call from my brother. "Mom died." My ticket was in my hand, my credit card was gone and of course I had returned my rental car. At first, I didn't know what to do, but then I realized she would have wanted me to go where I was most needed, and that was Cambodia. In a daze, I went through the security checkpoint.

My eldest son took my place at her funeral to speak the words that should have been my own. My children and my family respected my decision, even though they had a tough time grasping the level of my commitment to my work. I'll never be sure I made the right choice, or if the price of my commitment was too high.

My mother had said, "Why did you come from so far away? I'm just fine." Oddly, that's the exact opposite of what Freddy Quinn sings:

Come back soon, boy, come back home soon,

Boy, never go away again, never again.

I'm worried, worried about you,

Think also of tomorrow, and also of me.

Come back soon, boy, come back home soon,

Boy, never go away again, never again.

I've been an expat for nearly my entire professional life. I especially liked Cambodia, in an irrational way, for if you think of Cambodia in a rational way, it's no paradise. The poor are crushed by the powerful, corruption is far from being eradicated – the "cons" list is long. But so is the "pros" list. Cambodia, traversed by the Mekong, so rich with the Khmer culture and its marvellous temples – it radiates a magic, the people are endearing, they smile so much, and it's still a young nation, making progress in spite of all.

But I often felt homesick, and I missed my family and friends in France and the other countries I'd lived in. I had so much passion for my work in foreign countries and affection for their peoples, but this was all confused with the sense of what I was losing because of the miles that separated me from my "other" life, at home. For we expats sacrifice so much...

One day I said to myself, "You're like a wild orchid, with no other roots than those hanging in the air." I was wrong – the soil of our homeland always clings to our feet. And perhaps the reason this song, "Junge, komm bald wieder," moved me so much when I was young and throughout my wanderings was because it foretold those confused feelings I was to experience.

There, where voyages beyond the oceans led me in life,

I still remember what my mother wrote to me,

In every port, a letter came on board.

And she always wrote:

Don't stay so far away so long!

XI - Non-Governmental Organizations: Essential but Sometimes a Hindrance

Before going to Cambodia, I knew very little about non-governmental organizations, or NGOs, except what I'd read in the media when a humanitarian catastrophe calls attention to them, or during their funding campaigns when they send me pleas for donations.

But when I arrived in Cambodia in 1994, I immediately saw I would become familiar with this almost parallel world, known as the "blue world" because all license plates for NGO and IGO (international governmental organization) vehicles were blue. And most were Toyota 4WDs, universally popular with these agencies. Cars were a bit rare in Cambodia back then and were usually so dilapidated it was a miracle they ran at all, so these big brand-new 4WDs stood out wherever they went, emphasizing the humanitarian world's influence in the country. And there were a lot of those 4WDs.

I had never encountered IGOs or NGOs in my previous police cooperation missions to Morocco, Tunisia, Djibouti or other African nations, where I was busy training local officers and moved only in a circle of "official bilateral cooperation," so I had to catch up.

NGOs are a category of non-profit organization made up of private citizens, and depend on tax-exempt donations as well as governmental grants to do their work. NGOs can't enter into treaties or other international agreements, like IGOs, the most well-known being the United Nations.

When the UNTAC troops pulled out following the 1993 elections, they left in their wake a mass of NGOs that had begun to proliferate during its 2-year reign, having judged Cambodia stable enough to come back into and set up humanitarian aid. Practically all the UN agencies, such as UNICEF, coexisted in Phnom Penh along with several titans of international NGOs like Save the Children, Oxfam, Doctors of the World, Doctors Without Borders, Humanity & Inclusion and World Vision, along with more modest NGOs working to defend human rights, dig wells and build orphanages, schools and dispensaries.

Whatever the reason, geopolitical or – and this is conjecture on my part – guilt at having led or allowed Cambodia to sink into the horror of genocide, the Western world now opened its coffers to help the little kingdom, and the NGOs had only to ask to collect the subsidies.

Some countries, like the United States, avoid directly financing programs of governments they judge corrupt, incapable or authoritarian, so they funneled their donations through NGOs to promote their political priorities for Cambodia's development. And while many organizations depended on their own funds, for instance, with sponsorships to provide care for orphans, many others relied on contributions from international cooperation agencies or the support of a church or religious order – thus indirectly becoming agents for them. Meaning a sponsor's agenda could strongly influence an NGO's agenda. For example, donors would ignore an NGO's project if it did not include a component addressing HIV/AIDS prevention, so the keywords "AIDS components" would flourish in projects even if their designers had to tax their brains to figure out how to fit them in.

Naturally, humanitarians do as much as they can to finance the cause they're defending, but there are limits they should respect. Defining one's program with the sole aim of raking in funds, disguising a business as an NGO to benefit from tax breaks – those are the lines many people in the humanitarian sphere did not hesitate to cross, and with a serene conscience too, that of people who believe they're on the "good side" because they're defending good causes.

Along with its social and developmental programs, the blue world and its millions of dollars brought jobs directly or indirectly to thousands of Cambodians. This epoch, with Cambodia depending on money from the West, continues, and the NGOs' part in the economy is still important. The number of NGOs there is actually increasing – second only to Rwanda in the number of NGOs per capita. The Cooperation Committee for Cambodia[29] estimated

3,500 NGOs were present in 2013, and in 2022, there were more than 6,000. And according to the World Bank, about 1.37 billion dollars in international aid flowed into Cambodia in 2021 alone. All this despite a growing economy (7.7 % between 1998 and 2019) and a tsunami of billions in investments from China[30].

The first NGOs I got to know in Phnom Penh were LICADHO and ADHOC [31], whose members work to defend human rights, often in difficult conditions. People in trouble with the authorities naturally turned to these two NGOs for help, so as I began training investigative police officers in 1994, I contacted both for info on how the Khmer people considered the police and what obstacles I would face. They enlightened me as to the most critical deficiencies concerning the judicial system and the behavior of higher-ranking police, some of whom tended to forget the notions of "presumption of innocence" and impartiality of investigations. It was widely believed that anything was possible for rich, powerful personages and their friends, while the most severe penalties were reserved for the poor and weak. And before going after suspects, the police would find out who was behind them, who their clans and their supporters were. There were also major shortcomings in crime scene examination and the search for scientific evidence.

For all this and more, I decided to orient my judicial and technical courses to making the police force more efficient and impartial, and in so doing, contribute to protecting all citizens' rights.

A long period of cooperation with LICADHO and ADHOC ensued. They denounced violations and supported victims while I tried hard to make sure investigations respected the laws and followed the regulations and practices of a nation subject to the rule of law. After organizing the Project against child trafficking and sexual abuse, cooperation with these two NGOs became even closer and more operational.

I first entered the world of UN organizations – immense entities steered by executives of every nationality – when I began working on the UNESCO "Heritage Police" project to fight trafficking, theft and looting of cultural property. I learned the complexity of their procedures was only surpassed by the often-disproportionate ambitions of their programs.

I was proud to be a part of their project to protect the incredible archeological treasures of this little kingdom, formerly an empire. Only part of its cultural heritage has been discovered, identified and restored. The Angkor group of temples was protected, as it garnered so much attention, but many temples and monuments dispersed in the forest dozens of miles around this globally celebrated site were still enmeshed in the jungle. The most important were the Koh Ker and Beng Mealea temples. These were identified and opened to the public, while other sites were still inaccessible – except to looters.

Rubbing elbows with researchers, archeologists, and architects delighted to work in such an environment, and enthusiastic about their mission, was particularly interesting for me. I had the rare pleasure to visit Bayon with its many towers of enigmatic faces, Angkor Wat, Ta Prohm and other jewels of the Angkor complex, World Heritage sites all, in the company of eminent EFEO [32] scientists and their Cambodian partners. They were much more motivated than many local high authorities of the time, for whom the stone edifices were worth only the money they could slip into their pockets by charging admission to visit them, "when tourism exploded."

A highly determined French-speaking colonel, Chea Sophat, directed the Heritage Police. This permanent security force of 600 men patrolled the principal monuments and stopped the pillaging and degradation. My friend and colleague Georges Boltz and I helped train this force and oversee their work. Who can now say police and culture don't go together?

But I had still only touched the surface of the blue world. In 2000, when I became a UNICEF consultant on the LEASETC Project, I discovered the real multicultural universe of NGOs and IGOs, a world cohabited – not without a little squabbling – by well-paid senior officials and consultants, by volunteers and humanitarian workers paid a pittance but ready to give the shirts off their backs in exchange for a smile.

I attended regular follow-up meetings with the agencies[33] that supported and financed the Project, and whose representatives were expatriates from Canada, France, the U.S., the Netherlands, Japan, the Philippines, etc., and although we all shared a common tongue – English – it took me a while to understand the various accents. It was sometimes hard for my listeners to understand my imperfect English strangely tinted with a Franco-German accent. It also took me a while to adjust to the rites of certain NGOs. For example, World Vision staff meetings always began with a moment of silence then a short prayer and always wrapped up with delicious refreshments. I liked the relaxed and deeply humane ambiance of this NGO, one of the world's most important, with an annual budget of about 1 billion dollars in 2000, and about 3 billion dollars in 2021. Like UNICEF, World Vision backed the Project from start to finish and gave me boundless support and encouragement.

During our work meetings, time was not wasted on useless chatter. Our exchanges were frank, they respected my expertise, and when questions arose concerning the use of a budget or activity planning or rectifications, we always found a solution. Other organizations later joined this founding group, grafting a supplementary branch to the project. In addition to UNICEF, The Asia Foundation and several other NGOs furnished the know-how to produce our educational films on investigative methods, such as *Saving Seca*, and films needed for other purposes, like *The Victim* or *Your Move, Investigator!*

I never had any disagreeable incidents with these big organizations; however, with the "grassroots" NGOs, or those pretending to be, my experience was different. Overall, it was positive, but there were sticking points.

Before we launched the Project, a handful of NGOs had been the only recourse for sexual abuse or trafficking victims to find social, psychological and moral support. Among other reputable NGOs were Friends, Krousar Thmei, Pour un Sourire d'Enfants (PSE), Agir pour les Femmes en Situation Précaire (AFESIP) and Cambodian Women's Crisis Center (CWCC). "Friends" had been helping street children since 1994. Krousar Thmei, created in 1991 in a refugee camp on the Thai border, was well-known for assisting abandoned children, often victims of trafficking, and creating schools for deaf or blind children. This association's founder had always come to my aid when obstacles blocked my path. PSE helped children living in inhuman conditions in Phnom Penh dumping grounds, while AFESIP and CWCC gave shelter and a second chance to mistreated women or those who were exploited as prostitutes.

Around this same time, LICADHO and ADHOC had been working to apprise the authorities and international cooperation groups of how urgent it was to confront and contain human trafficking and exploitation. Their representatives reached into the four corners of the country, so the public was familiar with them and shared information and complaints. These "civil society organizations,[34]" or CSOs gave our newly constituted unit considerable help. Before we launched our hotline and even for some time afterwards, it was mainly through this avenue that cases pertaining to sexual exploitation of children were brought to our knowledge. They alerted us, handed over the elements they'd already gathered, and we launched our investigation.

We also turned to these NGOs to take in victims and provide material and psychological support for them. Rescue operations in a sexual exploitation setting, whether home, bar, or brothel, often take place at night, and we had no decent spot in our office, at least not at first, to accommodate the victims, even for a few hours. It's great to liberate a child from a brothel, but you also deprive him or her of a roof and a modicum of protection. The NGOs were the solution, all the more fitting because the children or young women found themselves surrounded by devoted people trained to interact with victims of crime.

But on occasion, NGOs went beyond their given role. One such incident occurred on a March morning when I got to my office and was surprised to see a six-foot-six Westerner filling a chair in my assistant's office taking notes on an active case implicating a foreigner. He did not belong to any official police service, so he should not have been privy to this kind of information. He was a member of a Christian NGO based in America, globally active in the struggle against pedophilia and other crimes against children. This NGO agent's intrusive attitude shocked me. I later met his boss, a former prosecutor I greatly respected, and he got things back to normal. It was essential that NGO members understand they could not access investigative files without permission from local judicial authorities, even if their staff members were highly competent legal experts. Afterwards, the Ministry signed conventions clearly delineating their role.

And that delineation was badly needed. In what I thought was an ill-advised act, in April 2003, the NGO in question helped organize and participate in a raid of Kilometer 11, the infamous red-light district in Svay Pak, earning for the NGO its hour of glory. The district had been closed down a few months earlier to "tidy up" Phnom Penh, which hosted the ASEAN summit that year, and the brothels discreetly resumed their activities behind the closed iron shutters of the city's myriad shophouses. About 60 police from the criminal investigation unit of the Phnom Penh headquarters had conducted the raids, helped out by some of the foreign "experts." They arrested twelve pimps and "rescued" about thirty underage prostitutes.

The police had not conducted a thorough investigation before this raid, relying on the detective work done by the NGO during the preceding two months, for example by infiltrating houses of prostitution to gather information and filming their premises with hidden cameras. Our unit was pushed aside, even though that was our specific area of competence, possibly because the municipal police resented us. Over time, senior officials in the ministry had come to consider our unit as a point of reference. Although created expressly for the protection of children, our growing capabilities in handling all types of sexual abuses, various forms of exploitation and trafficking of adults and minors had not escaped their attention. This did not please everyone. When the NGO so adroitly stepped in and delivered them a "turnkey" operation, the result was glowing media coverage for itself and Phnom Penh's criminal investigation police.

But from the point of view of the battle against prostitution, it was foolish, no matter how satisfactory the results appeared at first. Why? Having most brothels concentrated in Svay Pak meant it was easier to control. Making prostitution disappear from that one small area did not make prostitution disappear entirely; it only spread it out, which was bad for the police and for the women who worked there under duress. For all that, the intervention and resulting media coverage delighted the Cambodian Women's Affairs Minister. And I recognized, of course, that the image of this part of Svay Pak had been detrimental to the country, and how positive it was to show the police acting on a grand scale against prostitution.

Following the example of these Americans "on a mission," numerous NGOs led crusades against evil and sin. Their motivation might have been morally sincere, but that did not authorize them to intervene like a secondary police force. It seemed preferable to me, and I haven't changed my opinion, that they limit their interventions to giving material aid, equipment and training to local professionals to help them improve. It was like they were declaring, "You're no good, so we'll take care of it ourselves." My approach and that of the organizations supporting our Project was different: "Together, we'll find solutions best adapted to make progress, step by step." It may take more time, but the results will be longer-lasting.

Another reason that led humanitarian workers to step outside their accustomed role was their need for media exposure to attract financing. This concerned them all. I've seen associations founded to protect children from sexual predators turn to openly hunting pedophiles, almost pretending to be official law enforcement, seemingly unaware that leading a thorough criminal investigation, complete with surveillance and tailing, taking photos and searching houses, analyzing evidence in the lab, etc., is a matter for criminal investigators under a public prosecutor's control. It can make all the difference in putting pedocriminals behind bars or letting them go free.

This risk of seeing a case go off the rails was high when the race for results and the need for publicity drove NGOs to improperly mix themselves up in police affairs. One affair particularly shocked me.

An NGO had helped the police make two arrests, two weeks apart, in the same hotel. Going over the files, a troubling fact caught my attention: in both cases, although they were distinctly different, the victim was the same 14-year-old girl. As if she had served as bait. That changed nothing as to the perpetrators' criminal liability, but even so, can one justify endangering a child in order to trap a criminal – simply to mediatize the association's "heroic" work?

The NGO "investigators" denied any connivance, insisting that while monitoring the second delinquent they had not noticed he was with the same girl. That didn't convince me. Several times previously they had publicly declared, loud and clear, that they had no problem using provocation to catch those whom *a priori* they considered criminals. Without going so far as to call it a trap, isn't it possible this kind of technique could tempt a man who may never have crossed the red line into doing just so? The question must be asked. No matter how noble the cause, I'm against the whole business of investigators from outside the judicial system, working for NGOs that need to get "results" and subsequent media coverage in order to raise funds. Searching for leads or interviewing past victims is fine. Journalists do an excellent job of that, and the family members and friends of children at risk also participate in this by offering information or speaking of their suspicions. But all this data, these denunciations or tips should be communicated to the police, which should be the only entity empowered to carry out investigations, under the prosecutor's direction.

The affair of the Chai Hour II Hotel in the Tuol Kork area in Phnom Penh was one of the most telling as to how much some NGOs rely on the media for their funding and how negative a turn that dependence can take.

Journalists love a scoop, there's no denying. What's more delectable for a television crew than being in the center of the action, filming a police raid? It's not easy to do, though, unless they happen to be on the scene by chance or are invited by the police – or by an NGO in quest of media hype.

The NGO in question, AFESIP, informed the AHTJP department that minors were being sexually exploited in the Chai Hour II hotel, which features a restaurant, karaoke rooms, massage salons, VIP rooms for the mistresses of *Ta Ta* – rich, powerful, older men – and rooms for regular clients.

A two-month-long investigation by the NGO followed, and a few police officers from our department gave them a hand. Surveillance efforts brought no proof that either minors or women were being held against their will, so for me, there was no need to organize a raid. Suppressing sex services or "leisure" places themselves was not our priority. It would have been absurd to take aim at hotel pimping, as no hotel would refuse a room to a client accompanied by a "friend" or a client wanting a massage. Did we have to close them all down? Massage, even when accompanied by consensual sexual services, was not prohibited by Cambodian law.

Nevertheless, the NGO director Somaly Mam managed to convince General Un Sokunthea and General Hok Lundy to launch an operation to rescue 50 or so underage girls she claimed were in a state of misery inside the hotel. She also insisted the upcoming raid had to be conducted in the greatest secrecy on account of "the risk of complicity within the police force or accidental leaks."

I wasn't involved with the raid, as I was on duty near the Vietnamese frontier. Several casinos had been built there, and I needed to give additional training to the local special unit.

The operation took place late one afternoon in early December 2004. A couple dozen police from the AHTJP rushed into the hotel, accompanied by Mam and the other AFESIP leaders, a staff member from the prosecutor's office, and a French television crew. In the ensuing panic, about half the girls managed to run away, but 83 were "rescued," including masseuses, the *Ta Ta* mistresses and some hotel staff. Seven hotel management employees were also arrested. The intrepid television crew garnered some sensational images for a report on the NGO's courageous combat against the sexual slavery of Cambodian children by rich, powerful, corrupt men. The public got its money's worth.

However, something just wasn't right. The girls carried away didn't look underage, and their identity verifications later confirmed they were all over 18 except for one 17-year-old, who was not involved in sexual activities. There was only one conclusion: the NGO leader had lied to our unit chief. But the videos were a wrap and after all, what difference did it make? Those girls, minors or not, were "saved," right? I wasn't too sure about that. And now, they had no lodging. Our journalist friends got even luckier, for the drama was not over.

The police confided the young women to AFESIP, which was appropriate, as this NGO specialized in giving professional training to women who wanted to quit prostitution. However, their building was not set up to accommodate so many people. No matter, as long as the journalists could keep filming. AFESIP staff managed to feed the girls and put them up for the night as best they could. But as they had allowed the girls to keep their cell phones, they all called their friends, families and protectors, and in the small hours of the night, cars started to pull up in front of the building. The guards Mam had deployed had disappeared, and the girls rushed the door, dove into the cars awaiting them and hightailed it.

Mam announced to the media that armed men wearing military uniforms had descended on the center, broken down the gate and forcefully taken the girls after threatening the life of the director and all the personnel. Several witnesses and officers who conducted this "crime scene" would later say the gate had been forced from the inside and the girls had willingly departed. Whatever the truth was, our valiant Director Mam whipped up the media frenzy even further. She alerted the embassies, closed her center and left the country to "take refuge in Bangkok." There, she and her husband chose to attack the Cambodian authorities by criticizing the release of the seven suspects who had been arrested. Their release was questionable, but word had undoubtedly come down from the top to avoid making any influential *Ta Ta* a topic of public concern. Especially since nothing serious could be imputed to these rich men, unless keeping a consenting adult mistress was to be considered a crime.

The soap opera burst to life once more the following week, when some hotel employees and other women labeled prostitutes at the time of the arrest filed complaints for defamation and false imprisonment. And the next day, 50 of the "rescued" women protested in front of the American embassy, which had rushed to defend the NGO. When in turn their diplomats and those of other Western nations raised their voices against the government, saying it let the raid take place but then released the seven suspects, the government decided to create a commission to "establish the truth" behind this knotty affair. The immediate release of the suspects did cause problems. A normal 48-hour detention would have permitted the police to take their statements more conscientiously.

There would have been no Chai Hour II Hotel affair without the NGO's initial lie or exaggeration and its will to stage a media event with the complicity of a TV crew. The result? A police fiasco and a negation of Cambodia's genuine efforts to fight human trafficking. Even worse, Cambodia was placed on the U.S.'s "Tier 3" blacklist for countries least committed to fighting human trafficking. This was unjust, I believe, and especially disheartening to our unit chief, since her work put her on the front line of that combat every single day. She must have deeply regretted being duped that way, for her superiors reprimanded her for not having told them what she was preparing with AFESIP, the NGO in question.

Only this NGO came up a winner in this game of deception. Even though it had not "saved" a single sexually exploited child that day, AFESIP instantly built a reputation in international opinion as an organization fearless in its battle to liberate women from forced prostitution. Even "the big shots protected by the powerful and corrupt" could not shake its resolve. As a result, dollars poured in.

The project we had assembled with UNICEF and the other partners could have stalled at that point, but fortunately, the opposite happened. That fiasco had conclusively proved that the path we had chosen was the better one. Only by training police officers in the painstaking work of criminal investigation, with respect for procedure, could they garner real success. We also learned that an NGO's media or fund-raising agenda should never insinuate itself into our work.

XII - A Plea for the Regulation of Prostitution

After an extensive career in law enforcement, including those ten years in Cambodia committed body and soul to putting pedocriminals and human traffickers behind bars, I feel qualified to discuss prostitution. It is directly related because it too raises the fundamental issue of respect for a person's dignity and privacy concerning that one facet of human nature: sexuality.

I'm not talking about child prostitution, which should be fought relentlessly. All pedocriminals and all the recruiters, intermediaries, exploiters and clients of child prostitutes must be pursued, brought to justice and severely punished. Likewise, anyone – no matter how rich or powerful – who forces another adult directly or through threat or duplicity to sell his or her body in a brothel or anywhere else must be prosecuted before a judge and jury and do their time in prison.

That said, offering sexual services responds to a demand, almost entirely from men, a demand that will never cease. Some people in favor of "abolishing" prostitution claim that supply takes precedence over demand, and elicits it, arguing that if you suppress supply, demand will disappear. I don't believe that for a second. As long as humans are around, the need for sexual services – for prostitutes – will persist.

And that is exactly why prostitution should be regulated, not outlawed and relegated to the shadows, where there is only danger, abuse, misery, and the unhygienic conditions that lead to the propagation of disease. If this age-old service is to be exercised in good conditions, the public powers need to regulate it or at least keep some control over it.

"Regulated" prostitution presupposes a business relationship based on consent. The two adults freely commit to the sexual services to be bought and rendered, in locations approved by public health and social welfare authorities. Certain conditions would be guaranteed: hygiene, health and safety, age verification.

Sex workers would have a statute that protects them and offers them the possibility to manage not only their work hours, but their lives. Without a pimp, they could change course of their own free will or choose to remain a prostitute. There should be no shame attached.

The Thai government understands this. Thailand is one of the world's top destinations for sex tourism, and a regional marketplace for "sex workers," many of them Cambodian. Prostitution is not technically legal, but it is openly offered, condoned, and to make it easier for the police to control, it is restricted to certain parts of the big cities. In massage parlors and bars in these areas, you can meet many women, and men too, who propose sexual services without having been forced to do so by threats of violence.

When asked why they chose that life, many simply say it's their job and that thanks to the work, they can send money to their families or pay for their children's education. Most of their stories about how they ended up there are the same. A breakup, a divorce, a child to feed, poor parents, and presto, another sex worker in the market. This is not to say all women and girls undergoing such trials choose this path. Morals in Southeast Asia are not looser than anywhere else, contrary to the impression given by those who declaim the universality of paid sex acts there or the corruption of Asian women – these people ignore the hard reality of some women's lives. Most would prefer poverty over prostitution, which they consider degenerate. They would never tolerate selling their body.

But others do choose to sell their bodies, or at least resign themselves to it, and who are we to judge them based on our own moral values? Everyone has the right to decide what is acceptable or not in their life. Such a woman may ask herself, "Should I starve or live on the streets, or let my child or my parents suffer in poverty when the gifts I have – being pretty and attractive to men – could raise them out of it?" Putting moral considerations on one side of the scale and improving their income on the other, they decided the latter carried more weight.

Many Cambodian women who chose that life have misgivings, of course, especially about the question, "What will my family and neighbors think?" They could circumvent that issue by moving far away to Bangkok or Poipet for example and inventing a fictitious job in a foreign company or in a hotel chain. But their real work was prostitution.

By talking to many of these women in Bangkok I learned the "backstory" of this trade and how its regulation can lead to surprising outcomes. Their stories illustrate a type of commerce in sexual services that respects the people who practice it and helps them avoid the fate of street hustlers or prostitutes in a bar or under the thumb of a pimp.

I've been asked why I would seek out conversation with women in this profession. I had to if I was to be informed enough to express my opinion about sex workers. I needed to talk to them, listen to their stories, understand the paths that had brought them into their situation. So many absurd preconceived ideas circulate in the West about Asian women, that to eliminate them, we must be capable of empathy and compassion.

During all my years in Asia, I never isolated myself in expat circles, but sought encounters with the local population. I tried to adapt my methods, especially in training, to the local context. And I made an effort to meet people from all social strata, not just in Cambodia, where I lived from 1994 to 2010, but in other Asian countries like Thailand and Nepal, and while traveling in Malaysia, Myanmar, Vietnam and Bali. It was the same while conducting missions in Africa and Eastern Europe. It's always been easy for me to start conversations. I've long considered I have more to learn than to teach, especially in the philosophy of life. Perhaps that's why Buddhism practiced with wisdom and modesty influences my thoughts.

I don't smoke, I drink very little and almost never go to bars except on the rare occasion when I might accompany friends to please them, but even then, I prefer the terrace over a bar's closed space filled with smoke and jovial drinking. However, I enjoyed visiting massage parlors, ubiquitous in Asia, especially for a foot massage after long days of work, hours of shopping or visiting temples. Conversation came naturally with other clients while we sat waiting our turn, and with the massage therapists.

It also came naturally when I wanted to talk with the women in Bangkok who had chosen prostitution as their livelihood. I knew where to find them, as early every evening, these women crowd around tables in restaurants near their workplaces in the City of Angels[35].

I was sitting in one of these little restaurants just after sunset one day and noticed a group of four young women dining on soup, rice and small plates of fish, chicken and shrimp. By their clothing and behavior, I could tell they were sex workers. I figured I could engage them in conversation if I acted cheerful and relaxed – not like an uptight cop or missionary bent on redemption. I addressed them with a smile.

"That looks delicious. Would you mind ordering me a plate of *tom yum kung*, with a bowl of rice and a soda, please? I'm afraid the server doesn't understand me."

They laughed, and one of the girls called a server over and ordered for me. Then all four started firing questions at me: "Where do you come from? How long will you be here? Do you like massages?"

"I've lived in this part of Asia for a long time," I replied. "And where are you from, Cambodia? That's funny, as I speak a little Khmer." And so on, until we were all chatting about our lives. One of the women, Baaen, told me her story.

"I got married young, barely 17, and I was very much in love with Noy, my husband. He was ten years older than me and worked in a cell phone store. We lived in his uncle's house in Kampong Thom. My parents lived in a village about twelve miles away, on the road to Siem Reap. I soon got pregnant, and my husband started going out more often with his friends. He'd come home late, drunk, and as soon as I questioned him, he would get violent. In the last few months of my pregnancy, I went to live with my parents. At first, he came to see me every weekend, but one day I learned he was with another girl he liked better than me. We got divorced when our baby was born, and I never saw him again. Some people told me he'd gone to the Thai border to work in a casino. I was broken-hearted.

"So, I ended up alone with my little girl. We stayed with my parents, who had borrowed money to pay for my marriage and still had my two young sisters to raise. My father worked hard on construction sites and Mama took care of our little piece of land. We had chickens, two dogs and three beautiful mango trees that gave us shade and a lot of fruit. It was a wooden house on pilings, like nearly all the others there. We cooked under the house and slept on the upper floor on mats, protected with mosquito nets Mama stretched out like a tent.

"I knew my baby and I were too heavy an expense for them, and my dad was having a hard time holding off his debtors. But it was impossible to find work in the village. Finally, I got hired in Siem Reap as a server in a restaurant for 70 dollars a month including tips, so I was able to send 30 or so dollars to my parents. The boss let me eat with the others in the kitchen, but I had to pay 20 dollars to share a room with two other girls. I knew this would never do – it just wasn't enough. The interest on my parents' loans was like extortion, and even though they paid every month, their debts increased. I had to find a solution, or they would lose our little home. Then what would become of my sisters and my 1-year-old baby?

"That's when my friend Jorani, who worked with me at the restaurant, told me of an opportunity. Another friend of hers had found a job in Bangkok in a massage parlor, and this girl talked to her boss about us. He agreed to hire us for a trial period, and he would give us training. I desperately wanted to earn more money, enough to take care of my daughter, reimburse my parents' debts, and help give them a better life. I knew traditional massages wouldn't bring me much money and that I'd have to give the clients more than that to earn more. My friend and I talked about it, and we set our strategy.

"First, we wouldn't work in a bar, as bar girls have to drink alcohol with the customers, get hardly any sleep and lose their looks after a few years. And sometimes they get sick.

"Nor would we work in nightclubs, for the same reasons.

"We also decided we had to stick together, support each other and not hook up with any boyfriends, who we figured would live at our expense and cause us problems.

"As for massage and the extra services it sometimes leads to, I decided to fix my limits to some caresses and 'the happy ending,' nothing more. Besides, having sex is not allowed in my salon."

"What if the client invites you to his hotel after work?" I asked.

"That depends. In general, I do the same massage as in the salon, with a bit more service. I reserve 'full service' relations to the ones I like or who are extra generous. I want to protect myself and remain pretty and in good health. I want to stay within the limits I fixed for myself, because my goal is clear – earn as much money as I can, so I can change my life before I get too old and get pushed out on the street.

"What our boss wants is that the client is satisfied, gives a good tip and comes back. Of course, lots of clients request special massages, with perfumed oils, with, you know what—"

Giggles all around the table.

"—so we ask for them to pay more. That's where we can earn good money. A simple massage brings in only about 600 bahts a day, but with extra services, we can earn 1500 or even 2000 bahts in a day.

"I send money to my family every week, between 5000 to 7000 bahts. Mama uses what she needs and saves the rest to buy a plot of land and build a new house, a brick one."

"But what will you do when you have to leave this kind of life?"

"If I have enough money, it's easy, as I can get by alone or remarry. When you're rich, people respect you. Of course, we all dream of finding some rich foreigner who will give us a check every month, or even marry us. It's happened. But even that doesn't always work. Sometimes, the girl thinks only of getting money out of her *farang*[36]. In that case she wins, but the man is left penniless and unhappy about having believed in her. Sometimes, it's the foreigner who lies, and sends the money only once or twice, obliging the girl to go back to the massage parlor, sadder than before. Not to mention those who get into drinking or drugs and end their lives in squalor and degradation. That happens more often to bar girls. They're in a lot more danger than masseuses, and their bosses often exploit them.

"But I'm satisfied, as I have my friends and I earn enough to support myself and help my family. I don't think too much about the future. We're Buddhist, so we try to live in the present. I'm not saying we should forget about the future and preparing for it, and I do for the sake of my daughter, but it's better to concentrate on the present. I'm eating a delicious meal, I'm chatting with you, having fun with my friends, then I'm going to call my mama and talk to my daughter before she goes to sleep. Then I'll go to work. I'll smile, look flirtatious so a customer will choose me and give me a good tip. It's easy. I don't ask myself any other questions. Outside work, I dress like any other woman, take the bus or a taxi, do my shopping, take walks, drink coffee with friends. Then I go back to my work. I do go on vacation, but rarely, as crossing the border is risky. My situation here isn't exactly legal."

Baaen's story was like so many others I'd heard over the years. Her life was precarious, but she had had not been forced into prostitution, like so many others had as children or young adults, and she'd stuck to her choice. She did not seem to regret it.

I also heard some remarkable success stories from women like Kate Noknoi. A Thai native from the Isan region, Kate offered relaxation massages through an agency that sent their masseuses into hotels when clients contacted them by phone. She never knew who would be standing there when the door opened, or what she would encounter. To reduce risks, her boss only accepted customers from four- or five-star hotels, and before sending a girl, he got information about the client from the hotel receptionist.

In the intimacy of the client's room, Kate would strike up a conversation and quickly gauge whether to go beyond a simple massage. It was a question of "feeling," she explained, and money, of course. Being exceptionally pretty, slim and tall, she made an ideal partner for rich travelers who were alone in the immense city of Bangkok, and she often spent two or three nights with a client. She received half of what her boss billed the client and usually a generous tip for her services and company.

Kate worked for this massage escort agency for a few years, until she met a Dutchman who hired her for his whole stay, then paid her way to Holland to marry him. She learned his language, found work as a salesgirl and transformed her life. But she never forgot her origins, and her family kept its position in her heart. She assured me that if one day her marriage fell apart, she would still have her job, her statute as a legal resident in the Netherlands and the capacity to help her family. That was her true priority.

I knew of another girl like Kate, whose work in sexual services led her into a new life. Pom Chantana already had two children by the time she was 21, then she got divorced and left her village on the Mekong in northern Thailand. Like so many others, she went to work in a massage parlor in Phuket. The first was an ordinary salon where she earned about 400 dollars a month. Pom spoke English well, and she decided to bank on that. She hadn't come all that way south just to make enough to live on – she wanted more. And she got it when a client helped her get work in a highly select Japanese salon called Sakine Fashion Massage.

"It was a very discreet club, with tinted windows and a reception area with plush black sofas," she said. "We had a restaurant-style menu we would present to the client, listing our services and rates. They ranged from 1200 to 2400 bahts depending on the duration, services and number of 'hands.' Some clients wanted two masseuses, and some even hired three, so six hands would massage them.'

Pom said the words "Sexual Relations Prohibited" were displayed on the menu in big red letters, and the rule was respected. But this was mere semantics. Tantric and Kashmiri massage, erotic or nude massage – these were different expressions for the same "complete massage" offered in the salon.

Clients, men for the most part but sometimes couples, chose the service by consulting the brochure while Pom and her friends stood or sat on the other side of the room in full view, chatting among themselves, preening and hoping to be chosen.

"The Japanese were strict as far as hygiene and quite polite and proper," Pom pointed out. "However, their tastes were sometimes bizarre."

Non-Japanese clients were accepted in this club but had to respect the same rules: after undressing, they would place their affairs in a locker, shower, do a body scrub and then begin the rest of the program with a delicate massage using oils.

Pom worked there for six years, earning an average of 2000 dollars a month. Being thrifty and unencumbered with a "parasite fiancé," she sent all her extra money to her parents, as she could count on them to make good use of it. This was not always the case for children working far from home, as some parents would fall into gambling habits or alcohol abuse with this money "fallen from the sky."

At 28, Pom's address book was sufficiently full of clients – Japanese, American, European – to leave the club on the pretext of "going home to take care of her children." But in fact, she set up her own business in Bangkok, staying in touch with her contacts via social networks. They hired her to accompany them on their travels or to spend several days at a time with them on their vacations, and at a minimum rate of 600 dollars a week, and sometimes up to 1000, she earned a good living. A few of her habitués became friends, but for her, there was never a question of remarrying. Pom wanted to be a free woman.

"When I'm 40, we'll see. For now, what I want is to have a fun time in beautiful hotels with rich, generous men, often fairly old men, who like my company, my massages and my caresses. And I want to earn enough to ensure my future and my kids' education."

What could I rebuke her or her "clients" and friends for? There was nothing criminal about it. As for her fellow villagers, all they knew was that she worked in Bangkok for a Japanese company. Would they dare guess or gossip about the nature of her real activities now that she owned two large pieces of land, had enlarged her parents' home and built her own next to it? No, because money imposes respect, and not only in Asia.

Most girls in the sex-for-money industry have a more mixed experience though. This was the case with Rina Saengrun, who told me she had dreamed of a destiny like Kate's and Pom's, a life of freedom from worry about money. She grew up in Thailand near the Cambodian border in Surin, a village celebrated for its elephant festival, which attracts visitors from around the world to admire the remarkable shows, dances and games highlighting their intelligence and capabilities. Elephants, long the emblem of Thailand, are highly respected throughout southeast Asia. Rina was going to Surin to spend a week with her family, and I met her on the long bus ride to the festival. She ended up guiding my friend and me, so we didn't miss seeing hundreds of elephants performing acrobatics, marching, giving exhibitions of strength, battles and historical fresco simulations. On the bus and during the next few days, we learned all about her life and her hopes for a better future.

She fell into prostitution the same way Kate and Pom did, following the typical formula: a divorce with sole charge of her child, poor parents, a fruitless search for a decent job, a meeting with an intermediary, a debut in prostitution through a job in a tourist spa linked to a hotel center in Pattaya.

Rina described the job for me.

"At the start of our shift, the hostesses would sit on the steps of a room like an amphitheater, in the form of a half-circle. It was separated by an immense picture window from a room with sofas, tables and chairs, where clients could see us and choose at will. Like being in a fishbowl. Each of us had a number and wore a different-colored outfit, either blue, pink or black, according to our category depending on a girl's beauty, sexiness and customer demand for her type – the most expensive are called 'stars.' Sometimes groups of rowdy Chinese tourists crowded into the room, making jokes and drinking beer, then half the girls disappeared with them in rooms with jacuzzies and massage mattresses. The client got to choose the services and only the time was limited.

"I was considered one of the prettiest girls, so I was more expensive. That gave me a little protection from the most vulgar clients. A security team watched over us and made sure everything went all right and was done discreetly.

"For each service, half of the sum paid went to the boss for the room, products and other expenses. The other half was for the young woman. It was practically impossible to refuse a client unless you pretended to be sick or have your period or cramps. But it couldn't happen too often.

"I accepted my situation, and I was free to do whatever I wanted outside work hours, with one day off a week to shop and see my friends or take walks around the city. I could help my parents and I earned enough to cover the cost of educating my son. I was able to buy a moped and I thought I was happy enough with my lot. But deep down, I was disturbed. It wasn't having to sell my body for sex, but how hard it was to fix the limits on what I was ready to consent to, depending on the client and his mood. Because to my dismay the request for 'full service' came up frequently!"

She understood that in her workplace she could not easily set the limits she wanted to impose on her clients. How could she without losing her income? Luckily, after a few months, Rina met a Swiss tourist who hired her to stay with him for his entire visit, and after he left, he sent her money every month, enough to live on, and he returned to spend a few weeks with her twice a year. Since she was able to help her family, she quit the hostess job in Pattaya to live a simpler life and give up her dreams of wealth. She continued to provide massages, but only a few hours a day, leaving time to take care of her son.

In Cambodia, prostitution is formally prohibited but fairly tolerated; in Thailand it's prohibited too, but widely tolerated. These nuances vary from country to country around the world. In some places, remunerated sexual services are completely tolerated, taxed and regulated; others completely forbid it, including pimping, profiting from or encouraging the prostitution of others, and their laws are consistently enforced. French legislation is quite complex, and in my view, hypocritical. France and many other nations choose to consider prostitution a crime, not just for the prostitute but also the client. To me, this infringes on human rights – shouldn't two consenting adults be free to do whatever they want together? And in this era of the internet and online escort girls, the wealthiest men and women have the means to take advantage of top-of-the-line sexual services hidden from the eyes of the police, so they rarely get caught or punished. But average people are pursued, publicly shamed, and severely fined[37]. I don't think this is fair. Plus, the time spent by the police tracking down these clients could be better used in making sure the girls aren't working in dangerous conditions or under duress, and if they are, to hunt down those who are exploiting them. Even better, a more reasonable approach, regulating prostitution, would free up the police to concentrate more on protecting minors and ending human trafficking through international cooperation.

We live in a society of permissive morals, with our libertine clubs, partner-swapping and other fetching setups of a sexual nature, and I find it hypocritical to insist on considering prostitution – drawing an income from giving sexual satisfaction or pleasure – as an illicit activity. Beyond the moral issues and ideologies that impose their codes of conduct on individuals and brand with shame whatever their religious leaders find improper, we must remember the essence of the Universal Declaration of Human Rights of Man of 1948: every human being has the right to dignity as well as the right to freely choose the orientation of his or her life.

This Declaration, written by U.S. President Franklin D. Roosevelt when he was Chair of the United Nations Commission, has been signed by 192 nations. It has, of course, been used as an argument for and against prostitution, but I think Article 23 clearly supports my argument that a person should be able to choose it as a job without facing jail time: "Everyone has the right to work, to free choice of employment, to just and favorable conditions of work and to protection against unemployment."

Regulating prostitution could help ensure those "just and favorable conditions of work." So, let us be considerate rather than harsh, judgmental or vindictive when sex work involves consenting adults, and let our governments protect those who have chosen to engage in such work.

But let us be pitiless with criminal organizations that lure poor young girls into their nets by ruse, by force or through threats, who brutalize them, rape them, exploit them and ruin their lives; let us be pitiless toward all those who profit from that abominable trade in human beings.

I saw too many ruined lives during the years I helped lead the Cambodian project against human trafficking and sexual exploitation. In many cases, young girls had been sold to brothels in Phnom Penh or elsewhere and exploited for months, years, before they could be rescued, taken in by an NGO and cared for, then trained in another profession.

And we were often too late. Many other victims fell into total decay, alcohol, drugs, AIDS, and death. What choice did they have? Nobody wanted them anymore as a wife, not even poor laborers or tuk-tuk drivers. They could go back to the village penniless, covered with shame, and die there, or beg in the city streets until they perished from adulterated alcohol or a drug overdose – for they would do anything to forget and to stop the suffering.

Conclusion

Nothing Will Stop Cambodia's Struggle Against Child Trafficking

Saint-Raphael, France. In November 2021, I put away my notebooks and bulging files containing the documents, letters, papers, photos and newspaper clips about the cases and the subjects discussed in this book.

The stories, the faces, the dramas are so engraved in my memory, I could almost have done without those records. The stories have not been gathered here to show off my exploits, or profit in any way from the suffering of abused children. That would be inhuman. It simply made sense to share them and show how a program to fight sexual exploitation of children and to put their predators behind bars could be created from the ground up and make great strides against this vile practice. I was honored to take part in that struggle in Cambodia. And after all, protecting all people is stipulated in the priorities of the police institution, where I've spent my entire career.

When my mission in Cambodia ended in 2010, I put my years of experience to work by joining The Asia Foundation on a similar project in Nepal. I had every reason to believe the Project in Cambodia and its core ambitions would endure, because before I left, a new program, "Law Enforcement Advancing Protection of Children and Vulnerable Persons," or LEAP, was launched. LEAP would follow up on everything I had helped put into place, extend its field of action and continue assisting the Ministry of the Interior improve police protection of Cambodia's most vulnerable. LEAP's goals are the same: fight against sexual exploitation and abuse, domestic violence, human trafficking, abusive child labor, exploitative marriage brokering and adoption, drug abuse and issues confronting children in conflict with the law. This new program made it possible to pursue Project activities full speed ahead as well as to maintain a link with international partner organizations.

During my tenure, we had resolved thousands of cases of sexual exploitation and child trafficking, and worked patiently to integrate every unit associated with the Project into the national police system – the AHTJP at the national level and the ten special units based in the most relevant provinces. Besides aiding thousands of children and families, these achievements also helped Cambodia by improving its image as a nation taking steps to address this kind of crime.

And Cambodia desperately needed to maintain this specialized department because it had sorely lacked police intervention in exploitation cases. After its lengthy period of wars and massacres from 1970 to the early 90s, it had just opened its borders and entered a new, more peaceful era, although it was not until 1998 that the whole country was finally pacified. The presence on Cambodian soil of the Blue Berets from the United Nations and the opening of the country to the Western world have brought to this small kingdom, long cut off from the world, a substantial number of benefits.

However, certain perverse effects resulting from this rapid change had been noted, in particular an explosion in the number of places of prostitution: bars, dance halls, "biergarten" (some of which, like the Martini Bar, are still immensely popular). In 1994-1995, from 8 p.m. on, the capital, so busy during the daytime hours, fell into almost total darkness, except for the restaurants and especially the "relaxation places." They were always full.

The poverty of the population and the weakness of a judicial system based on a culture of impunity were certainly the main factors of the increase in Cambodia of prostitution, pedophilia, and the sexual exploitation of children since the beginning of the 1990s.

The LEASETC Project came into being in 2000, which I liked to call "Year One of the Fight" against sexual exploitation of children and the start of my association with that fight. It was also the start of big changes. The many pedocriminals we arrested in Cambodia during the period I've written about, of which I've narrated only a few examples, all shared a feeling of impunity – that in Cambodia they could do anything they desired. Before the Project came into being, they may have. But that has changed. Pedocriminals calculate the risks of being caught and put behind bars – and Cambodia's prisons are no joke. In a place where everything seems possible if you come armed with a few dollars, it might be "open bar" for perverts, but if the risk is high, they go elsewhere or are forced to use complex networks that protect them.

Investigations into pimping networks or prostitution houses marketing young children required more sophisticated investigation techniques than Cambodia possessed in the 90s. That became our special domain – to train police in surveillance, the collection of testimony and evidence that stand up in court, infiltrating an establishment or posing as customers, taking photographs and videos discreetly, collaborating with NGOs involved in child protection, etc. Over the years, the Project's units, integrated into the police system, succeeded at arresting many criminals and rescuing many victims. Some investigations failed, of course, for various reasons: an informer or accomplice within the team or the partner NGO, technical problems, false testimony, botched lab procedures. But little by little, techniques improved, and the number of failures decreased.

There were extremely difficult moments. Although a police officer my entire career, I still ached from the raw brutality of the crimes I had to confront there: raped children, trafficked babies. It changes you. One of the most painful sensations was seeing the expression of young victims trying to hide their shame or deep distress with an innocent smile. The sadness and shock in their eyes gave them away.

Police officers often try to dissimulate their emotions, too, by putting on a brave front or a brusque attitude, but I believe they remain sensitive to another person's distress. They need to – and not become like the people profiting from exploitation, hardened to the fact they ruin lives. And there were less obvious actors in this trade, "untouchables" like Cambodian *Okhna*, *Ta ta*, and others thinking themselves exempt – rich foreigners, diplomats and influential tourists. There were intangible obstacles to stamping out child sexual exploitation too, such as politics and the constant striving for power, defamation, revenge, jealousy, lack of motivation, misunderstandings, misinformation, and outside criticism. Or even mockery: "Watch out, here's the pedophile hunter!"

In the 1990s, owners of bars, karaoke or massage parlors simply needed a protector, often a high-ranking soldier or police officer, to operate with complete impunity. But things have changed. The fact we arrested the military police officer who raped the Canadian tourist in Sihanoukville shows that major change. We needed a great deal of perseverance to convince the authorities, to overcome the many obstacles, to visit the crime scene and gather the necessary evidence. But the hardest part was overcoming my partners' fear of attacking a man who wore a uniform.

It took specialized training of the officers to instigate a sea change like this, that nobody is above the law. That was the Project's first objective. Then we devoted time and money to develop new skills, create a database, a hotline, build new facilities and equip them, and as cases involving foreigners developed, we established links with legal authorities in neighboring and Western countries. That cooperation grew on a case-by-case basis, and I forged links, personal and official, with my German, French and American colleagues.

International cooperation with INTERPOL and other countries' police services was crucial, and from the early 90s, Cambodia also greatly benefited from a tidal wave of international aid. So many good intentions, and dollars to back them, so many hearts of gold. But there were a few problems, and despite the attempts of the Cambodian authorities to better supervise and regulate the status of NGOs, much remains to be done to sort the wheat from the chaff. The government and media opinion there now seems to suggest many NGOs should change their status to "commercial enterprise" to contribute more to Cambodia's long-term fiscal development. Some actually are businesses taking advantage of NGO status, and the worst are useless and parasitic associations. Some of them hindered our work in combatting sexual exploitation. That said, most NGOs there are motivated and effective and they're helping improve the living conditions of poor Cambodians.

As for my plea to regulate prostitution, I could have avoided this controversial subject and limited myself to writing only of the fight against trafficking and sexual exploitation of children. But I had to present my ideas on the delicate subject of prostitution, a word I dislike, preferring "sexual services." I condemn any form of exploitation, coercion or violence; however, I maintain that since paid sexual services exist and always will, everywhere in the world, it's far better these activities be organized in such a way as to ensure sex workers hygienic and safe conditions. Their work should also earn them social coverage, a place in society and as much dignity and freedom as other citizens enjoy. Their situation in Cambodia and elsewhere remains uncertain, but our program has lifted many to a better level.

Has our Project made Cambodia a haven of peace for sex workers, young women and children? Has it rid Cambodia of all pedophiles, rapists, and criminals who exploit them, sell them, abuse and even murder them? Sadly, no. Cambodia, like most nations today, will probably never be free of sexual abusers or traffickers of children. But thanks to this program I've written so much about, Cambodia has reduced its appeal for pedocriminals. And the efforts continue. After leaving the country, I followed the Cambodian news from Nepal, then from Thailand, then France, and over the years, I've read numerous articles about my former colleagues and my department's interventions to arrest sex criminals and about its prevention activities, especially in schools, to warn children of the dangers of pedophiles on the internet and social media.

My experiences and my reflections over the years eventually coalesced into this conclusion: a criminal phenomenon like the trafficking and sexual exploitation of children calls for the mobilization of all state departments and civil society as a whole. This mobilization is possible only if all those involved are motivated, sufficiently competent and possess the necessary material and financial means. Learning the law and acquiring expertise are easy; what is difficult is changing people's behavior and transforming the concept of professional ethics and public service as related to sexual exploitation in all its forms.

The wounds of the past are still visible in Cambodia, but young people want a better future, and one basic requirement for that is protection against destructive drugs, sexual trafficking and exploitation – the scourges that ruin their lives.

When I wrote the French edition of this book in 2021, I contacted several journalist friends who told me they were hearing fewer stories of sexual abuse of Cambodian children. They deduced from this that the situation was under control, thanks to the combined actions of the police services and social structures, among them the NGOs.

But since 2022, I've made half a dozen trips to Southeast Asia to promote the book and to study the evolution of pedocriminality and the drug trade, many of whose victims are children. I was able to get into contact with only a few of the police officers I'd trained, and no one could give me statistics that would allow me to get a real idea of the situation. Even my old colleagues and the UNICEF representatives I met did not follow up with solid information. I can only conclude that all these entities concerned with the crimes I want to continue researching were satisfied that sufficient services existed, and that "all was well." But I believe otherwise.

The current trend in Cambodia is to give great media coverage of drug dealer arrests and seizures to make everyone think the situation is under control. Drugs have become law enforcement's number one preoccupation. And young drug addicts will commit any number and any kind of infraction to find the money to get what they are slaves to. Including prostituting themselves for their fix.

I felt it was my duty to assist the government in fighting drug dealing and drug use among children, so in 2024, I provided a set of recommendations to set up a program to rescue child-addicts and help them break their addictions and also ways to dry up demand, but suddenly the whole idea was ditched. I was given no explanation, but I got the feeling I should let it go and stay away.

But to return to the evolution of pedocriminality and sexual exploitation, I will refer to the U.S.'s latest yearly report on the subject, and include an extract[38]:

> The Government of Cambodia does not fully meet the minimum standards for the elimination of trafficking and is not making significant efforts to do so, even considering the impact of the COVID-19 pandemic, if any, on its anti-trafficking capacity; therefore Cambodia remained on Tier 3.
>
> Despite the lack of significant efforts, the government took some steps to address trafficking, including investigating, prosecuting, and convicting more traffickers, creating a special working group to investigate credible reports of large-scale cyber scam operations involving indicators forced labor, and identifying and providing services for more Cambodian trafficking victims. However, corruption and official complicity in trafficking crimes, including by high-level senior officials, remained widespread and endemic, resulted in selective and politically motivated enforcement of laws, and inhibited law enforcement action during the year.
>
> Authorities did not investigate or hold criminally accountable any officials involved in widespread, credible reports of complicity, in particular with unscrupulous business owners who subjected thousands of men, women, and children throughout the country to human trafficking in cyber scam operations, entertainment establishments, and brick kilns.

Law enforcement did not effectively address forced labor in cyber scam operations. The government persistently failed to equitably screen or provide justice in trafficking crimes for foreign workers removed from cyber scam operations; it did not proactively screen them for human trafficking indicators. As a result, authorities did not provide or refer foreign potential victims of cyber scam operations to services, inappropriately penalized them for crimes committed as a direct result of being trafficked, including through holding these victims in indefinite detention until they paid bribes to police for release, or their foreign embassy funded their deportation.

This report may seem pessimistic, but it seems to me that in the visits I've made to Cambodia every year from 2021 to 2024, the program I helped launch some 20 years ago is still holding to its specific purpose and its integrity at the heart of the Cambodian national police force.

Some of the colleagues I'd been with since the beginning had been called to other missions by internal or external promotions, but others toiled on, like Lao Kimlin, a very young lieutenant when he joined us. I met up with him for a talk. He had been promoted to deputy director, and one of his missions was to make sure the unit kept up with the evolution of the crimes it was targeting.

"You see, *Uncle*[39], in Cambodia, just like the Philippines or Indonesia, pedophiles use the internet a great deal," Lao told me. "So we've created a new service to pinpoint cybercrime. We still use all the documents and tools you developed with us at the start of the Project – the pre-filled forms for procedural acts, certificates and medical expertise forms, the 'investigator's handbook,' the technical sheets on findings at the crime scene, warrants and searches, among others, but we've added a lot more and expanded our 'arsenal' to adapt to new forms of sexual criminality.

"Some pedocriminals still think nothing can happen to them here, no matter what they do. For instance, not long ago, an American who had abused several children offered to buy us a car if we would let him go. Instead, we put him behind bars, and then transferred him to the United States to serve a long sentence."

This incident sums up how well the Project accomplished what it set out to do. The pedophile sex tourist hit the "wall of zero tolerance" for child rapists, a wall of integrity I am proud to say I helped build. As a police officer, a parent and a concerned citizen, the motivation behind my commitment has always been to protect the weakest members of society. I'm even prouder that the professional and moral commitment of the men and women working on the Project is still going strong. It's just too bad UNICEF has not duplicated this project in other developing countries. It would be simple, because the hard work has already been done in Cambodia – an entire department, with a national and international network, built up from scratch, a special force highly successful at fighting sexual exploitation of children, at putting pedocriminals behind bars. UNICEF and its sister organizations should be setting these up all over the world.

On a personal level, though, the time and effort needed to fulfill my commitment cost me dearly. I was unable to be with my own children as much as I would have liked, and they were probably disappointed with me from time to time. My two youngest were still in high school when my wife and I separated, and I know they suffered from my absence. If I had been close by, I could have helped them through the ups and downs of life, not to mention being there to celebrate their birthdays and holidays together. I certainly can't blame them if they were disappointed. I never passed a day without thinking of them, though, and I never deceived them. After reading my book, I think they'll better understand, as they are fighters, too, successful in life due to their own efforts. They will understand I devoted myself to the Project so wholeheartedly because I felt a moral duty to aid suffering children, and I felt I could be most useful in Cambodia, in the struggle against pedophilia, a particularly abject crime.

An incessant and uncompromising struggle it was, and still is, not just in Cambodia but in every country of our world. Not just for law enforcement, for government entities, NGOs and IOs, but for all of us – it is our struggle, and only together can we succeed.

Acknowledgements

To Pierre Gillette, former editor of the French-language daily newspaper Cambodge Soir, which covered events in Cambodia from 1995 to 2007. I wish to thank Mr. Gillette for his encouragement and advice. We both spent many years in this country, animated by the same ideals in our respective domains of activity.

I also want to express my gratitude to Stéphanie Gée for her close reading of the original (French) version of my manuscript. And finally, many thanks to Galatea Laudouar, to have willingly taken on a surplus of work to produce the English version of this book. Teia encouraged me to participate in her work. We progressed from start to finish as a team, exchanging countless questions and ideas, adding phrases here and there, fine-tuning the original text to reach more English readers around the world and better share my experience with them.

Translator's Acknowledgements

Translating Mr. Guth's book was an arduous but valuable experience, and the first time I've worked directly with an author so unreservedly open to linguistic, aesthetic and creative suggestions. I especially appreciated Christian's prompt, detailed responses to my questions as we worked through such aspects of literary translation as cultural references, tone, chronology and modern writing tendencies. Together, we created a more global version of this important book.

[1]National United Front for an Independent, Neutral, Peaceful and Cooperative Cambodia, commonly referred to as FUNCINPEC. Prince Norodom Sihanouk founded this party in 1981 when he was in exile, to gather royalists that participated in the "anti-Vietnam Resistance" at the side of the Khmer Rouge and non-communist nationalists.

[2] Khmer is the word for the ethnicity and the language of the people of Cambodia and Cambodian is their nationality. The Kingdom of Cambodia is the official English name of the country, "Cambodia" being an anglicization of the French *Cambodge*, which in turn is the French transliteration of the Khmer ◇◇◇◇◇◇ (*Kâmpŭchéa*). A person from Cambodia can be called Khmer or Cambodian equally, but he or she speaks Khmer, not "Cambodian."

[3] Cambodia has used a dual-currency system since United Nations peacekeepers arrived to oversee elections in 1993, bringing U.S. dollars, which circulate in tandem with the official currency, the riel. As of 2022, the dollar remains the main currency, but the riel is becoming more widely used.

[4] Angkor, entered on UNESCO's World Heritage List, is one the main archeological sites in Southeast Asia. Spreading over 150 square miles partly covered in forest, the archeological park of Angkor contains splendid vestiges of the various Khmer Empire capitals that flourished from the ninth to the fifteenth century. The site's celebrated temple complex of Angkor Wat and the Bayon Temple are ornated with countless sculptures.

[5] Siem Reap ("the place where the Siamese were flattened") is the capital of the Siem Reap province, situated near Angkor, about 185 miles north of Phnom Penh.

[6] For reading ease, this Law Enforcement Against Sexual Exploitation and Trafficking of Children Project will be referred to from this point on as the LEASETC project or simply the 'Project.'

[7] Vietnamese word generally meaning a "madam" who organizes and supervises her prostitutes' work in a brothel or any other prostitution environment.

[8] A Cambodian, even though her name sounds Anglo-Saxon.

[9] *Le Cid* by Pierre Corneille, Act IV Scene III: "We were five hundred, but with swift support; Grew to three thousand as we reached the port,"

[10] Sole deep-water port in Cambodia, situated in the gulf of Thailand. Little frequented at that time, the seaside town and its coves of fine sand on the edge of a turquoise sea offered a décor worthy of a post card to its residents and visitors.

[11] One riel is worth about 0.125 dollars, so a shoeshine cost just over a dime.

[12] *Lok kru* is a polite designation for a person who taught you something. "The student" continues to use the term for life.

[13] Tenement-style residence typical of commercial areas in Cambodian towns, long and narrow like a shoebox, with a ground floor that serves as a shop during the day and garage for a car or motorcycles at night, with the residence on the floor above.

[14] Popular onomatopoeia for coitus.

[15] "Ass."

[16] In 1999, Cambodia joined this group, better known as ASEAN, of nine countries: Indonesia, Malaysia, the Philippines, Brunei, Singapore, Thailand, Myanmar, Vietnam and Laos.

[17] An Apsara is a celestial dancer in Buddhist and Hinduist mythology. Gifted with supernatural beauty, elegance and grace, superb at dancing, and she plays the role of mediator between heaven and earth.

[18] "Westerner" in Khmer.

[19] International Criminal Police Organization, or INTERPOL, with 195 member nations is the world's largest police organization. It does not have the power to make arrests but enables police to work directly with their counterparts, even between countries that do not have diplomatic relations.

[20] Once a title accorded by the king to a mandarin, with accompanying responsibilities and privileges. The *Oknha* of today, numbering in the hundreds, are mainly businessmen the government rewards with this distinction for their "generous contributions to the nation's development." To the average Cambodian, an *Oknha*, whose arrogance is at times limitless, is often seen as an unscrupulous (and untouchable?) man who bought his title in exchange for his "generosity," so the authorities not only leave his business alone but protect him.

[21] *Srey* is a word used before a girl's name, meaning "young girl or "young daughter" or "Miss."

[22] Capital of the Banteay Meanchey province in northwestern Cambodia.

[23] About 50 dollars, or 1 dollar for 30 baht.

[24] *Tết Nguyên Đán*, or Vietnamese New Year, celebrated between mid-January and the end of February according to the dates fixed by the lunar calendar.

[25] The 1991 Paris Peace Accords led to the establishment of the United Nations Transitional Authority in Cambodia, whose mandate was, among other things, to maintain peace and prepare for elections. To this end, some 21,000 Blue Berets (also known as Blue Helmets) were deployed in the country as peacekeepers until the elections were held in 1993.

[26] Gendarmes are locally known as MPs or "Military Police." They belong to the Royal Cambodian Gendarmerie, a branch of the Royal Cambodian Armed Forces and are responsible for the maintenance of public order and internal security in Cambodia.

[27] My sphere of action included the national Anti-Human Trafficking and Juvenile Protection Department and the six busiest provincial units, one of which was in the capital.

[28] Popular open-air restaurants, inexpensive, often animated by live music, where beer with ice is served by "beer girls," young women wearing uniforms with the brewery or distributor's label to promote the brand.

[29] One of five committees of the Parliamentary Assembly of the Francophonie (APF).

[30] Per the Taiwanese website Doublethink, which indexes 36 nations' exposure to Chinese influence and disinformation, Cambodia is ranked the world's "most exposed" to Chinese influence, based on scores on a wide range of factors, including military, politics, academia and technology. (https://china-index.io/country/Cambodia.)

[31] The Cambodian Human Rights and Development Association, the country's oldest human rights organization, founded by a group of former political prisoners.

[32] The French School of the Far East, or École Françoise d'Extrême-Orient, abbreviated EFEO, is an associated college of PSL University dedicated to the study of Asian societies. It was founded in 1900 with headquarters in Hanoi in what was then French Indochina.

[33] IOM, World vision, Save the Children Norway NL, Terre des Hommes, Kamonohashi.

[34] The term "CSO" includes non-governmental organizations, public and private foundations, professional organizations, labor unions, as well as cooperatives and economic operators whose main objectives define them as social enterprises.

[35] A translation of the Thai name for Bangkok, Krung Thep, which is an abbreviation for the official name Krung Thep Maha Nakron, itself an abbreviation of the full ceremonial name containing twenty-two words, including "the great city of angels."

[36] Word for Westerner in Thai.

[37] Up to 1500 euros in France, for example.

[38]   https://www.state.gov/reports/2023-trafficking-in-persons-report/cambodia/

[39] Polite word English-speaking Cambodians use to address a foreigner of their parents' generation.

About the Author

With over four decades in law enforcement in Europe, Africa and SE Asia, Christian Guth is uniquely qualified to write about fighting crime. He lives in the south of France, but travels extensively, lecturing about sexual predation of children "to awaken sleeping consciences to this plague of human society."

Read more at christian-guth.com.